Giovanna Magi

ALL PARIS

in 130 photos in colour

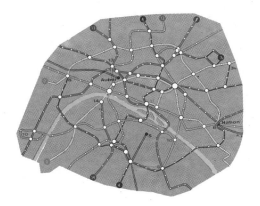

ƎB
BONECHI PUBLISHERS

All the photographs
in this book were taken by
JACQUELINE GUILLOT, Paris

Translated from the Italian by
MICHAEL HOLLINGWORTH

ISBN 88-7009-055-8

Printed in Italy

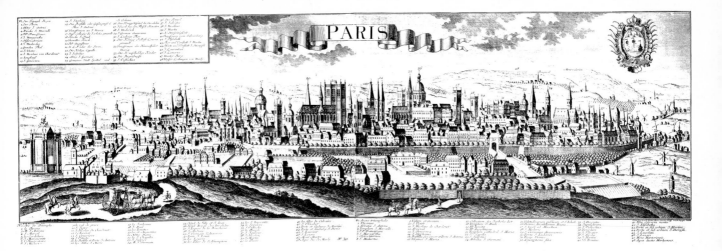

HISTORICAL NOTE

Writing a brief historical outline of Paris is no easy task: few cities have been so involved in great events which have changed the course of history. Its founders were probably the Gauls, who built a small settlement on the left bank of the Seine. The Romans reached here at an early stage, led by Julius Caesar, who in his " Gallic Wars " repeatedly mentions the town under the name of Lutetia. As a result of the continued and increasingly serious threat of the barbarian invasions, the original settlement was transferred to the island called Ile-de-la-Cité, from which point a slow but continuous expansion on both banks of the river began. The simple residence first of the Merovingian then of the Carolingian kings, Paris became a true capital in the year 987 when Ugo Capeto founded a new dynasty, raising the city to a status it was to retain throughout the entire course of the history of France. From this moment, Paris began to develop not only as an urban centre, but also from the cultural point of view. The accession to the throne of Philippe II Auguste, who reigned from 1180 to 1223, marked the beginning of one of Paris's most splendid periods: the construction of the Louvre was begun and in 1215 the University was founded. New splendour came with the reign of Louis IX (Louis the Blessed), which lasted from 1226 to 1270 and during which the Sainte-Chapelle was built and work on Nôtre-Dame considerably advanced. Under the following dynasty, that of the Valois, Paris experienced one of the most bitter periods in its history: 1358 was the year of the revolt headed by the leader of the Parisian merchants, Etienne Marcel. Charles V re-established order, being responsible among other things

for the construction of the Bastille, but the peace did not last. The civil war waged between the Armagnac and Burgundian factions permitted the occupation of France by England, Henry VI being crowned King of France in Nôtre-Dame in 1430. Finally, in 1437, Charles VII reconquered Paris but there were renewed internecine struggles and increasingly bloody revolts, alternating with terrible epidemics of the plague, which devastated the already distressed population. Then, throughout the 16th century, the importance of Paris was diminished in favour of the castles of the Loire, which the various kings who succeeded to the throne of France chose as their dwellings. This did nothing to put a halt to the internecine strife in the capital itself. The spread of the Protestant movement lay at the origin of the bloody religious struggles which for a long time rent Paris and France, culminating in the massacre of the Huguenots on 24 August 1572, the famous Night of St. Bartholomew. After the assassination of Henry III at St. Cloud by the young Jacques Clément in 1589, the city was besieged for four long years until it opened its gates to Henry IV, who had abandoned his original faith and been converted to Catholicism. All the same, at the beginning of the 17th century Paris already had a population of 300,000 persons. The city continued to grow in importance as a cultural and political centre, above all under the powerful Cardinal Richelieu, who in 1635 founded the Académie Française. During the new dynasty of the Bourbons, the city expanded even more: by 1715, during the reign of Louis XIV, it had half a million inhabitants. But Paris without doubt gained its place in history in 1789 with the beginning of the French Revolution, often seen as marking the birth of the modern world. Usually the Revolution is considered to have begun on 14 July of that year, when the people seized possession of that symbol of absolutism and terror, the prison of the Bastille. During the years which ensued, the historical developments came in ever more rapid succession: the monarchy fell, the Reign of Terror began, to be followed by the Thermidorian reaction, and in a short period of time the figures which had dominated the Parisian political scene disappeared for ever. What the city had suffered during those years (the loss of human life and the irreparable destruction of works of art) was forgotten with the advent of the Empire and the magnificent court which Napoleon created in 1804, when he was crowned in Nôtre-Dame by Pope Pius VII. From 1804 to 1814 the city was embellished with one artistic masterpiece after another: the column was erected in Place Vendôme, the Arch of Triumph was built and work continued on the Louvre, where in the luxurious Salon Carré in 1810 the marriage between Napoleon and Marie Louise of Austria was celebrated. Later again, Paris saw the fall of other monarchies, those of Charles X and Louis Philippe Bourbon-Orléans, and the birth of the Second Republic with the rise to the throne of Napoleon III. It was during the reign of the latter that Baron Haussman

was given the task of replanning the city, thus solving the difficult problem of traffic which was already choking the French capital. The markets of Les Halles were constructed, the parks of the Bois de Boulogne and the Bois de Vincennes were designed, the Opéra was built and the main boulevards were reorganised.

In 1870, the defeat suffered by Napoleon III at Sedan at the hands of the Prussians led to the revolt of the Parisians, which in turn initiated another unhappy moment in the history of the city, the period of the Commune (18 March-22 May 1871). Many beautiful and historic buildings were unfortunately destroyed in this period of rebellion, among others the splendid Hôtel de Ville and the Tuileries. But at the beginning of the 20th century, Paris saw a new rise to splendour, with the World Fairs held there, the construction of the Grand Palais and the Petit Palais, and the birth of its new artistic movements, both in painting and in literature. Sad to say, the city had yet to suffer in two more long and bloody wars, which brought bombardments and ruins. In the second world war, it was taken by the German Army in 1940 and liberated by the Allies only in 1944. From that moment on, however, returning to its tradition as a free city full of life, Paris has retained its place in the history of mankind and its culture.

NOTRE-DAME

Built on the site of a Christian basilica which had been occupied previously by a temple dating from Roman times, the church was begun in 1163 under Bishop Maurice de Sully, work commencing from the choir. As time passed the nave and aisles followed, and finally the façade was completed in about 1200 by Bishop Eudes de Sully, though the towers were not finished until 1245. The builders then turned to the construction of the chapels in the aisles and in the choir, under the direction of the architect Jean de Chelles. In about 1250 another façade, that of the north arm of the transept, was completed, while the façade on the south arm was begun some eight years later. The church could be said to be finished in 1345. With the ravages of time and damages caused by men and by numerous tragic wars, the church's original appearance changed over the centuries, especially during the Revolution: in fact, in 1793 it ran the risk of being demolished. Nôtre-Dame at that point was dedicated

to the Goddess of Reason, when Robespierre introduced this cult. But it was reconsecrated in 1802, in time for the pomp and ceremony of the coronation of Napoleon I by Pope Pius VII in 1804. It underwent a definitive restoration by Viollet-le-Duc between 1844 and 1864, and it was threatened with destruction by fire in 1871. Imposing and majestic in its stylistic and formal consistency, the façade of Nôtre-Dame is divided vertically by pilasters into three parts and also divided horizontally by galleries into three sections, the lowest of which has three deep portals. Above this is the so-called Gallery of the Kings, with twenty-eight statues representing the kings of Israel and of Judaea. The Parisian people, who saw in them images of the hated French kings, pulled down the statues in 1793, but during the works of restoration at a later stage they were put back in their original place. The central section has two grandiose mullioned windows, on each side of the rose-window, which dates

from 1220-1225 and is nearly 33 feet in diameter. This central section is also adorned by statues of the Madonna and Child and angels in the centre and of Adam and Eve at the sides. Above this runs a gallery of narrow, intertwined arch motifs, linking the two towers at the sides which were never completed but which, even without their spires, have a picturesque and fascinating quality with their tall mullioned windows. Here Viollet-le-Duc gave free rein to his imagination: he created an unreal world of demons who look down with ironic or pensive expressions on the distant city below, of birds with fantastic and imaginary forms, of the grotesque figures of leering monsters, emerging from the most disparate and unlikely points of the cathedral. Crouching on a Gothic pinnacle, half-hidden by a spire or hanging from the extension of a wall, these petrified figures seem to have been here for centuries, immobile, meditating on the destiny of the human race which swarms below them.

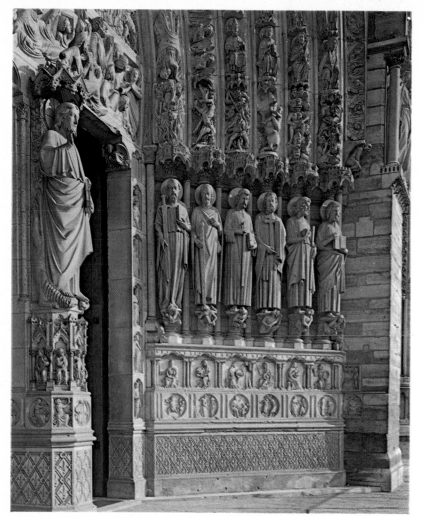

Detail of the portal

The Gothic style of these portals (dating from about 1220) is characterised by a softer and more direct way of looking at and interpreting nature, whereby the material is used to create more delicate forms and the space between one figure and another is more freely distributed. On the central portal is the subject perhaps best loved by the Gothic artists, that is, the Last Judgment. On the pilaster which divides it in two is the figure of Christ, while on the embrasures are panels with personifications of the vices and virtues and statues of the Apostles. Figures depicting the celestial court, Paradise and Hell are sculpted with great skill around the curve of the arch. The lunette with the Last Judgment is divided into three sections and is dominated by the fig-

ure of Christ, at whose sides are the Madonna, St. John and angels with symbols of the Passion. Beneath this on one side are the blessed who have merited salvation, and on the other side the damned being dragged towards their final punishment. In the lower strip is the Resurrection. The right-hand portal, called the Portal of St. Anne and built between 1160 and 1170, has reliefs dating from the 12th and 13th centuries, with a statue of St. Marcel, bishop of Paris in the 5th century, on the pilaster which divides it. In the lunette Our Lady is depicted between two angels and on the two sides are Bishop Maurice de Sully and King Louis VII. The third portal, the one on the left, is called the Portal of the Virgin and is perhaps the finest of the three because of its epic tone and the solemn grandeur of its sculpture. On the dividing pilaster

is a Madonna and Child, a modern work. In the lunette above are the subjects dear to the iconography of the life of the Virgin, including her death, glorification and assumption. At the sides of the portal are figures depicting the months of the year, while in the embrasures are figures of saints and angels.

Interior

Entering the interior of the cathedral, one is immediately struck above all by its dimensions: no less than 426 feet long, 164 feet wide and 115 feet high, it can accommodate as many as 9000 persons. Cylindrical piers 16 feet in diameter divide the church into five aisles, and there is a double ambulatory around the transept and choir. A gallery with double openings runs around the apse above the arcades, being surmounted in turn by the ample windows from which a tranquil light enters the church. Chapels rich in art-works from the 17th and 18th centuries line the aisles up to the transverse arm of the transept. At each end of the transept are rose-windows containing splendid stained-glass pieces dating from the 13th century; particularly outstanding is the stained-glass window of the north arm, dating from about 1250, with scenes from the Old Testament and a Madonna and Child in the centre, justly celebrated for the marvellous blue tones which it radiates. From the transept one passes into the choir, at the entrance to which are two piers; the pier on the north has the famous statue of Nôtre-Dame-de-Paris, dating from the 14th century and brought here from the Chapel of St. Aignan. An 18th-century carved wooden choir surrounds half of the presbytery, and on the high altar is a statue of the Pietà by Nicolas Coustou; at the sides of this are two more statues, one representing Louis XIII by Giullaume Cousteau and the other Louis XIV by Coysevox. Finally there is the ambulatory with radial chapels which contain numerous tombs. On the right, between the Chapelle Saint-Denis and the Chapelle Sainte-Madeleine, is the en-

trance to the Treasury, in which can be seen relics and sacred silverware. Among the most important relics are a fragment of the True Cross, the Crown of Thorns and the Sacred Nail. At this point, having reached the end of the church, if one turns towards the main entrance one cannot help being struck by the great rose-window above the 18th-century organ, in which are depicted the signs of the zodiac with images of the months and of the vices and virtues.

Interior: south rose-window

A work of the 13th century, but restored in the 18th century, it depicts Christ in the act of benediction surrounded by apostles and the wise virgins and foolish virgins. The richness and luminosity of the colours and the precise placing of the glass tesserae combine to give almost the impression that a single, intensely bright star is bursting, throwing its splendid rays of light in every direction.

Apse

From the bridge called Pont de la Tournelle, constructed in 1370 but rebuilt many times, one can see the vast curve of the apse of Nôtre-Dame. In other churches, the part centring on the apse usually aims at gathering together, as if in an embrace, all the lines of force and the rhythmic and spatial values of the interior. But here the apse creates its own rhythm, serving as a terminal point but also creating a new sense of movement which extends to every structural element, from the rampant arches to the ribbing. The rampant arches, which here reach a radius of nearly 50 feet, are the work of Jean Ravy.

Right side of the Cathedral

An evocative view of the right side of the cathedral can be had from the colourful quay of Montebello, one of those streets along the Seine always so full of animated life. The " bouquinistes ", the famous sellers of prints old and new where rare and curious books can also be found, give this street its peculiar flavour and typical Parisian spirit.

LA CONCIERGERIE

This severe and imposing building on the banks of the Seine dates from the time of Philip the Fair, that is between the end of the 13th and the beginning of the 14th centuries. Its name derives from " concierge ", name of the royal governor who was in charge of the building. Today it constitutes a wing of the Palais de Justice. A visit to the castle is of considerable interest, since it is full of memories and takes the visitor back to distant and troubled times of conspiracy and revolution. In fact, from the 16th century on it served as a state prison. Then, during the Revolution, its cells were occupied by thousands of citizens who lived out their last hours here before climbing the steps to the guillotine. On the ground floor is the Hall of the Guards, with power-ful piers supporting Gothic vaults, and the large Hall of the Men-at-Arms. The latter room, which has four aisles and is no less than 224 feet long, 88 feet wide and 26 feet high, was once the dining-hall of the king. From the nearby kitchens the expert cooks of the royal house were capable of preparing meals for at least a thousand guests. To speak of the Conciergerie, however, takes us above all back to the time of the Revolution; visiting the cells and learning the segrets of the building we are following the last footsteps of those condemned to death, many of whose names are only too well known. In a large room on the ground floor, with cruciform vaults, the prisoners could have, for a certain fee, a straw pallet on which to sleep; in another area, with the tragically ironic name of Rue de Paris, the poor prisoners were quartered. The cell of Marie Antoinette, convert-ed into a chapel in 1816 by the only remaining daughter of Louis XVI, the Duchess of Angoulême, is perhaps the most evocative of all: here the royal prisoner, scornfully called the " Austrian woman ", lived from 2 August 1793 until 16 October; on this Wednesday morn-ing, at 7 o'clock, after cutting her own hair, she too climbed on the cart to be taken to the scaffold where nine months before her hus-band had died.

SAINTE CHAPELLE

From the courtyard of the Palais de Justice, through a vaulted pas-sageway, one reaches that master-piece of Gothic architecture which is the Sainte Chapelle. It was built for Louis IX (Louis the Blessed) to contain the relic of the crown of thorns which the king had bought

in Venice in 1239; the relic had been brought to Venice from Constantinople. The architect who planned the chapel was probably Pierre de Montreuil, the architect of Saint Germain des Prés; here he actually designed two chapels, standing one above the other, and they were consecrated in 1248. The lower church acts as a high base for the overall structure, above it being large windows crowned with cusps. The steep sloping roof is adorned by a slim and delicate marble balustrade, and this graceful piece of architecture is splendidly crowned by a slender openwork spire 246 feet high. Two more towers with spires stand on each side of the façade, in front of which is a porch; above the porch is a large rose-window with cusps, dating from the end of the 15th century, its subject illustrating the Apocalypse. The whole work is marked by its lightness: the structural elements lose their consistency to become subtle embroidery, delicate lacework. The ribbing becomes slender, the pinnacles finer, until the architecture almost disappears, leaving only the huge stained-glass windows.

SAINTE CHAPELLE
Lower Church

There is without doubt a sudden change of atmosphere, style and emotion when one descends from the Upper to the Lower Chapel.

Only 23 feet high, it has three aisles, but the nave is enormous compared to the two much smaller aisles at the sides. Trilobate arch motifs supported by shafts recur along the walls. The apse at the end is polygonal. But here too, as in the Upper Chapel, it is the colour which predominates. The rich polychrome decoration overshadows the architecture, which is thus transformed into a simple support for the decorative element.

SAINTE CHAPELLE
Upper Church

Climbing a staircase from the Lower Chapel, one reaches the Upper Chapel, a splendid reliquary

with the appearance of a precious jewel-case. Without aisles, it is 55 feet wide and 67 feet high. A high plinth runs all around the church, interrupted by perforated marble arcades which from time to time open up onto deep niches. In the third bay are the two niches reserved for the king and his family. On each pillar is a 14th-century statue of an Apostle. The architecture is thus lightened as much as possible in order to leave room for the huge stained-glass windows, nearly 50 feet high. Whereas in the art of the Romanesque period a church's paintings had been half-hidden in an apse, in the curve of an arch or under a wide vault, here in this Gothic creation the pictures are magnificently transferred to the stained-glass windows, triumphantly presented to the gaze of all and illuminating the whole church with their precious colours. The fifteen stained-glass windows of the Sainte Chapelle, belonging to the 13th century, contain 1134 scenes and cover an area of 6650 square feet; they illustrate, in splendid colours and in an excited, almost feverish style, Biblical and Evangelical scenes.

PONT NEUF

Despite its name, which means "New Bridge", the Pont Neuf, designed by Du Cerceau and Des Illes, is the oldest bridge in Paris: it was begun in 1578 under Henry III and completed under Henry IV in 1606. From the point of view of its design, however, it is decidedly a "new" bridge, indeed revolutionary compared with previous designs. All the other bridges in the city, in fact, had had tall houses built on the sides, hiding the view of the river. Here instead a perspective on the Seine was created and the bridge, with its two round arches, became an enormous balcony thrust out over the river. The Parisians appreciated its beauty and importance at once, and the bridge became a meeting place and favourite promenade. At the beginning of the 17th century, it even saw the birth of the French comic theatre, when the famous Tabarin gave his performances here.

SQUARE DU VERT-GALANT

Known by the nickname given to Henry IV, " Vert-Galant ", this pleasant little square is reached via a stairway behind the statue of the king. Here one is actually at the end of the Cité, and at this point the comparison of it with the prow of a ship comes spontane-ously. The garden occupying the square, in fact, thrusts out over the calm waters of the Seine like the bows of a ship ploughing the waves. The landscape which opens up before one here is among the most evocative offered by the city: the visitor is in almost direct contact with the river, and in one vast sweep his gaze takes in the majestic banks, the graceful buildings, the green of the trees and the elegant outlines of the bridges.

STATUE OF HENRY IV

François-Fréderic Lemot erected this equestrian statue dedicated to Henry IV in 1818, to replace the previous work by Giambologna which had been placed here when Maria de' Medici was queen, after the assassination of Henry IV in 1610, but torn down in 1792.

INSTITUTE OF FRANCE

Linked to the Louvre by the picturesque Pont des Arts, the first bridge built of iron, this building was erected in 1665 as the result of a bequest by Cardinal Mazzarino who in 1661, three days before his death, stipulated in his will that two million francs be spent on the construction of a college capable of accommodating 60 students, to be called the College of the Four Nations. In 1806 Napoleon ordered the transfer here of the Institute of France, which had been formed in 1795 by the union of five academies: the Academies of France, of the Sciences, of Letters, of Fine Arts and of Moral and Political Sciences. The commission for designing the building was given to Le Vau, who took the Roman Baroque edifices as his model. The façade of the central section has columns which support a pediment, above which is a fine cupola with the insignia of Mazzarino sculpted on its drum. This section is linked to the pavilions at either side by two curving wings with two orders of pillars. Entering the courtyard, one can visit on the left the Mazzarino Library and on the right the formal Meetings Room: here, beneath the cupola, in what was originally the college chapel, are held the solemn ceremonies for the presentation of new members of the French Academy. In the vestibule preceding this room is the tomb of Mazzarino, a work done by Coysevox in 1689.

HÔTEL DE VILLE

In the centre of a huge square which for five centuries was the site of public executions is the venerable Hôtel de Ville, today the municipal headquarters of the city. On the site which it occupies there was previously a 16th-century building, designed by Domenico da Cortona: built in the Renaissance style, it was destroyed by fire in 1871, during the struggles which led to the fall of the Commune. The later building thus takes its inspiration from this lost edifice. It was designed by the architects Deperthes and Ballu, who completed it in 1882. The complex is certainly imposing and original, with its various pavilions surmounted by domes in the shape of truncated pyramids and with a forest of statues in every angle. In fact, there are no less than 136 statues on the four façades of the building, while on the terrace is the statue depicting Etienne Marcel, leader of the Parisian marchants and fomenter of the disorders which crippled Paris in the 14th century. Over the centuries the building has been the scene of important historical events. The most tragic of all, perhaps, took place on the morning of 27 July 1794, the day which in the new calendar created by the Republicans was called the 9th of Thermidor. Robespierre, the Incorruptible, was closed inside the Hôtel with his followers, trying to find a way of avoiding the threat of a civil war which he knew would certainly create havoc among the factions that had emerged within the Republican system. When the soldiers of the Convention burst into the room, Robespierre tried to commit suicide by shoot himself in the throat, but he succeeded only in inflicting a jaw wound. He was dragged off, to be executed the following day.

TOUR
ST. JACQUES

Occupied today by two meteorological stations, this is all that remains of the ancient church of St.-Jacques-la-Boucherie, destroyed in 1797. Erected between 1508 and 1522, it is 170 feet high and belongs to the most elaborate Gothic style. Narrow windows alternate with niches crowned by spires and pinnacles, in which there are many statues. The statue at the top of the tower of St. James the Greater is by Chenillon (1870). Another statue, this one depicting Pascal, stands at the base of the tower under the vaults as a reminder of his barometric experiments in 1648.

PLACE
DES VICTOIRES

This square, circular in form, came into being in 1685 as a surrounding for the allegorical statue of Louis XIV, commissioned from Desjardins by the Duke de la Feuillade. The statue, destroyed during the Revolution in 1792, was replaced in 1822 with another in bronze by Bosio. Under the direction of the architect Jules Hardouin-Mansart, the square was built up in such a way that all the buildings had the same monumental style, thereby creating a genuinely outstanding uniformity and stylistic unity. Important figures in the life of France came to live here, among them the Duke de la Feuillade himself, who occupied numbers 2 and 4, and the financier Crozat who lived at no. 3. Today only the buildings from number 4 to number 12 remain: the others were altered in the following centuries, so that they lost their original style.

GARDENS OF THE PALAIS ROYAL

This palace, built by Lemercier between 1624 and 1645, was originally the private residence of Cardinal Richelieu, who bequeathed it on his death in 1642 to Louis XIII. Today the seat of the Council of State, it has a colonnaded façade erected in 1774 and a small courtyard, from which one passes through a double colonnade into its beautiful and famous garden. The garden, planned in 1781 by Louis, extends for nearly 250 yards, with green elms and lime-trees and a profusion of statues. It is surrounded on three sides by robust pillars and a portico which today accommodates interesting shops with antiques and rare books. During the Revolution it became a meeting-place for patriots: here the anti-monarchist aristocrats, among them the Duke of Orléans who was later to be rebaptised Philippe Egalité, met to discuss the state of the country and the historical developments about to be unleashed. In these gardens, in front of the Café Foy to be exact, on 12 July 1789, Camille Desmoulins harangued the crowd, inflaming them with his passionate speech. Later, he was to tear a green leaf from one of these trees and put it in his hat as a cockade. The crowd followed his example and two days later, at the storming of the Bastille, many wore the leaf emblem.

PLACE DES PYRAMIDES

Along Rue de Rivoli, almost at the level of the Pavillon de Marsan, is the small, rectangular square called Place des Pyramides, which has buildings with porticoes on three sides. In the centre of the square is the equestrian statue of Joan of Arc, a work done by Frémiet in 1874 which attracts pilgrimages every year.

ST. GERMAIN L'AUXERROIS

In front of the eastern part of the Louvre is a small square dominated by the symmetrical façades of the Mairie, or town-hall, of Paris's First Arrondissement, dating from 1859, and of the church of St. Germain l'Auxerrois. The two buildings are separated by a bell-tower, built in the neo-Gothic style in 1860. Also called the "Grande Paroisse", the Great Parish Church, because it was the royal chapel of the Louvre in the 14th century, St. Germain l'Auxerrois stands on the site of a previous sanctuary dating from the Merovingian era. Its construction was begun in the 12th century and continued until the 16th. On the façade is a deep porch built between 1435 and 1439 in the Gothic style, with five arches, each one different from the others, its pillars adorned by statues. Other statues, depicting saints and kings, are in the three portals. Higher up is a fine rose-window surmounted by a cusp, next to which is the church's bell-tower dating from the 11th century. The sight of the interior of the church is impressive: it has five aisles, divided by piers, transept and choir. It also contains numerous works of art, among which a worthy example is the royal pew which F. Mercier carved from wood in 1682. Also in polychrome wood is the statue depicting St. Germain, while the statue of St. Vincent is of stone but it too is enlivened by the use of warm colours. Both these works date from the 15th century. Among other works of art worth mentioning is a Flemish reredos in carved wood, the scenes of which depict moments in the life of Jesus.

THE LOUVRE

LOUVRE The Colonnade

Before this colonnade was built, the minister at the time, Colbert, summoned Bernini from Rome, and in 1665 the great Italian artist presented a plan which was clearly Baroque in flavour. Since this did not correspond to the tastes of the French court, which was already inclining towards neo-classical forms in which a reverence for the ancient world and an academic culture could be felt, the project was then entrusted to Claude Perrault, who between 1667 and 1673 directed the erection of this famous monumental colonnade. Made up of extremely tall twin columns, for which Perrault used iron reinforcement, the long gallery runs along a high base, interrupted by windows. Three architectural masses, of which the central one is crowned by a pediment, project from the façade. The motif of two opposing L's, surrounded by garlands within a medallion, which recurs along the façade, is the seal of Louis XIV.

History of the palace and museum

The origin of the Louvre dates back to the 13th century, when Philippe Auguste had a fortress built near the river for defensive purposes: the fortress occupied about a quarter of what is now the Cour Carrée, or Square Courtyard. Not yet a royal dwelling (in fact the king preferred to live on the Ile de la Cité), the fortress contained within its sturdy walls the royal treasury and archives. In the 14th century, Charles V, known as Charles the Wise, made the building more inhabitable and converted it into his royal residence; among other things he ordered the construction of the famous Librairie, meriting for this work alone the historic appellative by which he is known. After his reign, however, the Louvre was not to be used as a royal palace until 1546, when Francis I commissioned the architect Pierre Lescot to carry out alterations and extensions which would adapt it more to the tastes of the Renaissance. To do so, Lescot had the old fortress demolished and the new palace erected on its foundations. Work continued under Henry II, still under the direction of Lescot who, for the sculpture, had the collaboration of Jean Goujon. After the death in a tournament of Henry II, his widow, Caterina de' Medici, entrusted Philibert Delorme with the task of constructing the Tuileries Palace and uniting it to the Louvre by means of a long wing which extended towards the Seine. Work was interrupted on the death of Delorme, but resumed and completed under Henry IV, who had the Pavillon de Flore built. The building was further enlarged under Louis XIII and Louis XIV, with the completion of the Cour Carrée, which because of the wealth of its sculptural decorations became the most distinguished part of the so-called Old Louvre, and the building of the east façade with the colonnade. When the royal court was transferred to Versailles in 1682, work was virtually abandoned and the Louvre fell into such a state of ruin that in 1750 its demolition was even considered. It could be said that the women of the Parisian markets saved the building when, with their march on Versailles on 6 October 1789, they forced the royal family to return to Paris. After the tormented years of the Revolution, work on the building was eventually resumed by Napoleon, whose architects Percier and Fontaine began the construction of the north wing, finished in 1852 by Napoleon III, who finally decided to complete the Louvre. After the fire which destroyed the Tuileries in May 1871, the Louvre assumed the appearance which it still has today.

Following the dispersion of the important Librairie of Charles the Wise, it was Francis I in the 16th century who began a collection of art works, the first nucleus of what was to become one of the most important collections in the world. This was considerably enlarged under Louis XIII and Louis XIV, and indeed by the time the latter died the Louvre was regularly the scene of exhibitions of painting and sculpture. Finally, on 10 August 1793, the gallery was opened to the public and thus became a museum. From then on, the collection was continuously enlarged, not least by Napoleon I who demanded a tribute in works of art from the nations he conquered. The objects contained in the museum's catalogue today amount to about 400,000, subdivided into their various sections which range from ancient Egyptian, Greek and Roman works to those from the Orient, from medieval to modern sculpture, and objets d'art such as those belonging to the Royal Treasury to the immense collections of paintings.

LOUVRE - Square Courtyard and Clock Pavilion

This grandiose courtyard, more than 390 feet long on each side, was originally the enclosure in the early castle built by Philippe Auguste. The buildings here reveal various phases of construction, but the most interesting part is without doubt the central pavilion, built by Pierre Lescot and consisting of two orders of windows surmounted by an attic. The whole façade of this wing was also richly decorated with statues and reliefs by Jean Goujon and his school. In the centre of the wing is the Clock Pavilion, designed by Lemercier under Louis XIII; its construction, begun in 1624, was made possible by the demolition of the " Librairie " Tower, part of the Louvre as it was at the time of Charles V. At a later time, during the Restoration, the clock visible today was erected in place of a previous window, while the sculptors Buyster, Poissant and Guérin were responsible for the powerful caryatids standing below the cupola. Louis le Vau designed the other three wings of the courtyard, which originally had two floors though these were later increased to three by Percier and Fontaine, the architects of Napoleon I.

CARROUSEL ARCH

Designed by Pierre-François Fontaine and Charles Percier and built between 1806 and 1808, it celebrates the victories of Napoleon Bonaparte in 1805. It could be said to be an imitation of the Arch of Septimius Severus in Rome, repeating as it does that monument's architecture and plastic decoration. Red and white marble columns frame the three vaults and each front is filled with bas-reliefs which recall the Emperor's victories. On top of it were placed the four gilded horses which were removed by order of Napoleon from the Venetian basilica of S. Marco, to which they were returned in 1815. The originals were then replaced with copies, to which a chariot and the statue of Peace were later added.

LOUVRE
The Denon Pavilion

The pavilion, at the centre of which is the main entry to the Louvre Museum, is surmounted by a quadrangular cupola and is remarkable for its luxurious decorations of statues, caryatids and reliefs. Above the arches of a portico runs a terrace filled with statues depicting illustrious men.

Mesopotamian Art
Standing figure of Gudea

Among the extant neo-Sumerian statues, which stylistically are a continuation of the preceding period under the dynasty of Akkad, are about 30 works depicting Gudea, the " patesi " of the city of Lagash. The Sumerians used the name " patesi " to indicate a dignitary who occupied both a political and religious position: Gudea refused the title of king and would accept only this designation. Most of the statuettes were found during excavations by the French at Tello. Gudea is depicted in both sitting and standing positions, but in each work his hands are joined in the act of prayer. This is one of the most famous and finest of the statuettes because of its simplicity and intense religious spirit; made from dolerite, it is 41 inches high. The figure has a typical Persian lamb's wool hat on the head and a simple cloak on the shoulders. Acquired by the Louvre in 1953, it belongs to the " high-dynastic " era, that is between about 2290 and 2255 B.C.

Persian Art
The King of Persia's Archers

These famous archers, made from enamelled brickwork (since Mesopotamia had very little stone, its buildings were constructed from bricks baked in the sun and then enamelled), are the so-called Immortals, the private guard of the King. The archers, each one 60 inches high, make up an endless procession covering the walls of the luxurious palace of Darius at Susa. The archers differ from one another in minute details, and this almost monotonous repetition of the same figure gives the impression of endless, uninterrupted movement. Their stately and dignified poses and the brilliant colours of their clothing make them a sort of hymn celebrating the greatness and might of the Persian Empire. They belong to the 5th century B.C., the time of the Achmenides dynasty, whose dominions extended for almost two centuries throughout the entire Middle East.

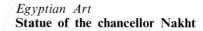

Statue of the chancellor Nakht

Found during the excavations of
Assiut, this statue belongs to the
Middle Kingdom at the time of the
13th Dynasty, when Egypt, under
the rule of the energetic Theban
kings, had a period of great power
and prosperity. As a consequence,
its art too was stimulated and went
on to new conquests. This surpris-
ingly realistic statue, made of wood
on which can still be seen traces of
the original colour, represents the
chancellor Nakht. It is in a rigidly
frontal position, although there is
a hint of movement in the left leg
which is slightly forward of the
body. The almost nonchalant position of the right hand, hidden in a
fold or pocket of the long cloak,
gives the figure an unusually natural
and spontaneous quality.

Egyptian Art
Seated Scribe

Found in 1921 near Saqqârah in an excavation project directed by Mariette, the Scribe is a masterpiece among Egyptian statues. It belongs to the Old Empire, that is to the time of the 5th Dynasty, and was presumably made in about 2500 B.C. It is 21 inches high and is made of painted limestone, with eyes of semi-precious stones: the cornea is of white quartz, the iris of rock crystal and the pupil of ebony. The Scribe's fixed stare, the rigidly geometric composition and the severely frontal stance of the massive figure are its most obvious features. At the same time, it is animated by an intense sense of internal life: the Scribe seems to interrogate the spectator with his eyes, ready to begin work on the roll of papyrus which rests on his knees.

Greek Art
Exaltation of the Flower

Most of the works of Greek statuary have unfortunately been lost to us, and we know them only through late imitations and Roman copies. But in this room are exhibited original archaic works (dating, that is, from between the second half of the 7th century and the beginning of the 5th century B.C.). Outstanding among them for its beauty and elegance is this Exaltation of the Flower, in which can barely be seen the gentle smiles of the two maidens, from whose arms, linked as if in a dance, the flower and fruit of the pomegranate emerge.

Hellenistic Art
Venus de Milo

Discovered in 1820 by a peasant on the island of Milo in the Cyclades, this statue has come to be considered the prototype of Greek feminine beauty. Somewhat more than 6 feet high, with its arms broken off (no one has ever succeeded in establishing what the original position of the arms was), it belongs to the Hellenistic Age, that is to the end of the 2nd century B.C., but it almost certainly derives from an original by Praxiteles. Like the other works by this great sculptor, the figure is slightly off balance, as if resting on an imaginary support, which gives a delicate curve and twisting movement to the bust. Critics and art lovers have long gazed on the slender nude body of the goddess emerging from the heavy cloth of her cloak which is slipping towards the ground. The material of the statue itself, Parian marble, gives the goddess's body and skin a lightness worthy of the finest classical traditions.

Michelangelo (1475-1564)
Prisoners

Sculpted between 1513 and 1520 for the base of the tomb of Pope Julius II (which was never completed), these statues were given to Henry II of France in 1550 by the Florentine exile Roberto Strozzi. Later they were transferred to the castle of Anne de Montmorency, at Ecouen, and then to that of Richelieu, finally reaching Paris where they came to the Louvre at the time of the Revolution. In Michelangelo's symbolic terms, they were perhaps meant to represent the Arts, imprisoned by Death after the death of the pope who had for so long been their protector. Above all, however, they are the clearest and most powerful expression of the restless, tormented spirit of Michelangelo in his unceasing effort to dominate the material of his art.

Hellenistic Art
Nike of Samothrace

Found in 1863 at Samothrace, with the head and arms missing (one hand was discovered in 1950), this work dates from about 190 B.C., a period when the inhabitants of Rhodes had a series of military victories against Antioch III. The Nike (or Victory figure) stands erect on the prow of the ship which she will guide to victory: the sea wind hits her with all its force, tearing at her clothing and pressing it to her body. The clothing here is treated in an almost Baroque way (which would fully justify the rather late date assigned to the work): it vibrates in contact with the Victory's body and flaps in the wind, which in turn pushes the Victory's arms violently backwards. About 9 feet high and made from Parian marble, this is without doubt one of the most important works of the entire range of Hellenistic statuary.

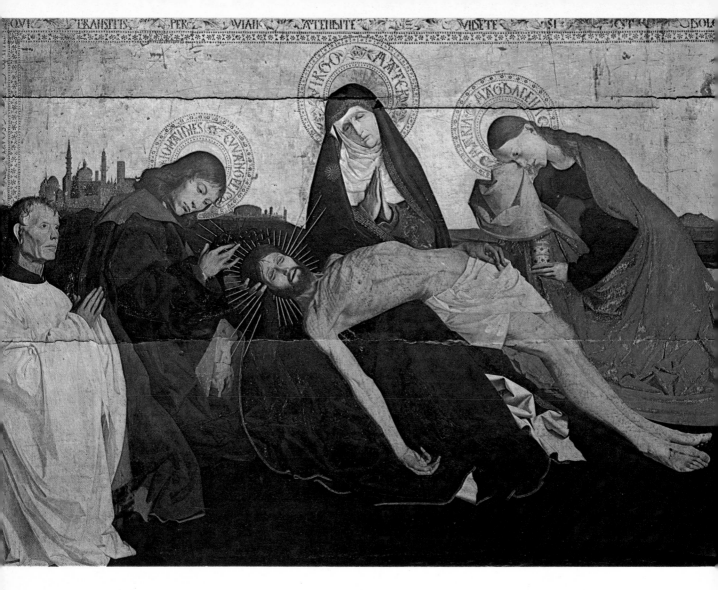

School of Avignon
Villeneuve-lès-Avignon Pietà

This splendid panel, a genuine masterpiece of the Gothic International style, saved from a fire in 1793 and rediscovered in 1801 in the church of Villeneuve-lès-Avignon, has long presented a problem as to both its dating and attribution. Some critics have advanced the name of Enguerrand Quarton because of certain iconographical details, while others have said that it is the work of a Spanish painter, if not actually derived from Van der Weyden. The group stands out powerfully against the gold background which is the last remaining heritage of the Gothic style and will soon be replaced by compact

blue skies. The figures seem to be derived from the numerous Pietà sculpted in ivory, wood and stone. The colour contrast is splendid, while the body of Christ is abandoned on the knees of the Virgin and St. John, his face remarkably expressive, removes the thorns from Christ's head. According to some critics, the figure on the left of the panel, representing the donor, is the canon Jean de Montagnac. A strong sense of pathos and profound emotion is created by the horizontal line of Christ's body, which tragically interrupts the static and compact group surrounding it. The sure sense of design and above all the expression of dignified grief seen on the faces of the figures make this panel one of the masterpieces of French painting.

Jean Fouquet (c. 1420-c. 1480)
**Portrait of Charles VII,
King of France**

This painting, hung in the Salon Carré where the marriage of Napoleon I and Marie Louise was held in 1810, is a justly famous work by Jean Fouquet, and seems to have been done in about the year 1444, that is shortly after the painter's trip to Italy. The painting was given by the king to the Sainte Chapelle of Bourges, where it may have remained until 1757, the year in which the church was demolished. It entered the collection of the Louvre in 1838. It offers a three-quarter view of the king, richly dressed and standing out clearly against the background.

School of Fontainebleau
**The Duchess of Villars
and Gabrielle d'Estrée**

The unmistakeable style of Clouet is fairly obvious in this work, attributed to the School of Fontainebleau, which can be dated at around the years 1594-1596. This is another example of the portrait, a genre which by then had become a fashion much patronised in court circles. Between the heavy curtains behind the two women a glimpse of domestic life is given: a woman sitting beside the fire, busy with her sewing. The two female figures, whose portraits have been painted while they are taking a bath together, are two

sisters, Gabrielle d'Estrée and the Duchess of Villars. The latter, with a symbolic gesture, is announcing the future birth of the son of Gabrielle, who was the mistress of King Henry IV.

Georges de la Tour (1593-1652)
Mary Magdalene with Oil-lamp

The artistic formation of George de la Tour, who was born at Vic-sur-Seille and died at Lunéville, was rather complicated. He preferred compact, closed volumes and a pure geometric style, forms immersed in the shadows and revealed by skilfully placed rays of light. It is obvious that he learnt much from

Caravaggio. According to some critics, the Caravaggio influence derived from a trip to Rome which the painter made around the year 1612 or 1613; other critics believe the technique came from the artist's contacts with the works of Gherardo of the Nights, another painter fascinated by the problem of light and shade which he resolved with surprising ability. This painting, done towards 1635 or 1640, is full of a sense of desperate solitude, expressed in the way Mary Magdalene stares abstractedly at the tiny flame, which seems to be consumed before our very eyes, and in her almost mechanical way of caressing the skull in her lap.

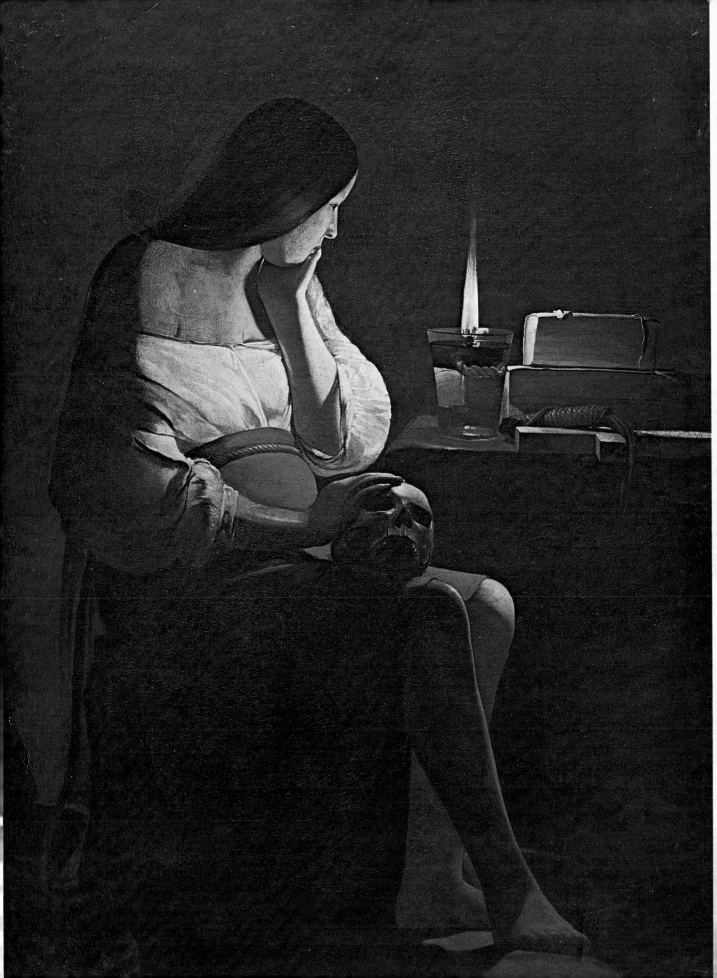

Nicolas Pouissin (1594-1665)
Rape of the Sabine Women

Born in France, Poussin passed many years of his life in Rome, where he died. Here the painter came into contact not only with the Baroque world, which was slowly coming into being, but also with the world of the late Renaissance, which still survived in the works of Raphael in the Vatican. Poussin preferred to paint large works of a mythological or historical sort, like this Rape of the Sabine Women, of which he also painted another version, now in the Metropolitan Museum of New York and datable at around 1637, that is some years after the work in the Louvre. Typical of Poussin's painting is the sense of agitation which can be felt

between the figures, so strikingly framed in the motionless setting of classical architecture.

Claude Lorrain (1600-1682)
Campo Vaccino in Rome

Like Poussin, Claude Gellée, better known by the name of Claude Lorrain, also lived for many years in Rome. His Roman landscapes are full of a warm, golden light, typical of those sleepy afternoons when the shadows grow to enormous lengths on the rough terrain of the Roman Forum. With the eyes of one passionately interested in the antique world and its remains, Lorrain allowed his gaze to rest on a broken pediment, an arch covered at the top with moss, columns lying full-length on the ground, overturned

capitals. His way of seeing nature and interpreting the landscape was thus completely different from that of Poussin.

Louis Le Nain (1593?-1648)
Peasant Family

Of the three Le Nain brothers, Antoine, Louis and Mathieu, Louis is considered without doubt the best artist. A painter who specialised in portraying rustic scenes and lovingly recorded the world of the humble people, far from the luxuries of the court, he too displays in his work a distant echo of the luminous technique of Caravaggio, painting dark interiors with a minimum of illumination. But what was a metaphysical, supernatural light in Caravaggio is transformed in Le Nain's work into the quiet

glow of the fireplace. The members of this poor peasant household seem to have been posed in front of an imaginary photographer, each one having left off his normal activity. The painter, more than ever poetic in this work, captures the tiniest details of the room with affection and accuracy, dwelling on it with a feeling of lament for a pure and simple world.

Philippe de Champaigne (1602-1674)
Ex-voto dated 1662

Deriving from the Jansenist beliefs of the artist, this panel is painted according to the iconographical tradition of the ex-voto and represents the painter's daughter, Sister Cathérine de Champaigne, abbess of Port-Royal des Champs, as she is miraculously cured of paralysis after the prayers of Sister Cathérine Agnèse Arnaud. The event is described in the Latin epigraph on the left of the panel, and there is an air of mystic sanctity in the serene and dignified expressions on the faces of the two nuns. The painting, signed and dated, was done between 22 January and 15 June 1662.

Charles Le Brun (1619-1690)
The chancellor Séguier

An architect as well as painter, Charles Le Brun was head of the French Academy during the reign of Louis XIV. In fact he decorated most of the Palace of Versailles and the sketches for its plastic decorations are also his work. His style clearly takes its inspiration from the Italian artists of the 16th century, in the richness and opulence of the clothing, in the stately quality of the poses and in the rich, warm colour. Here Le Brun has portrayed Pierre Séguier, Chancellor of France and the painter's patron during his youth. The painting may have been done towards 1655 or 1657.

François Boucher (1703-1770)
Diana resting after leaving her bath

A typical representative of the French Rococo style, Bouchet was a court painter at the time of Louis XV and enjoyed the patronage of Madame la Pompadour. His is a festive, refined art, full of the joy of living. Rather than war-like divinities, he preferred painting more seductive figures from mythology, and this is why the many paintings of Venus which he left have been called « boudoir Venuses ». The female bodies which he loved to paint are perfectly proportioned, in the triumphant nudity of adolescence, warmed by his tenuous and delicate colours.

Antoine Watteau (1684-1721)
Gilles

If Rubens is the highest expression of the Baroque Age, Watteau is without doubt his equivalent in the era of Rococo. Rather than the unleashed passions in the great Flemish painter's work, Watteau depicts an intimate, idyllic world. Done around 1717 or 1719, this work represents Gilles or Pierrot, a character from the Italian Commedia dell'Arte, and the figures in the background also belong to the popular theatre. The painting was acquired in 1804 by Baron Vivant-Denon from the art dealer Meunier, who had it displayed as a signboard for his shop in Place du Carrousel. In 1869 it was bequeathed to the Louvre. One critic, Mantz, has suggested that the work is a portrait of the comedian Bianconelli. In any case, the painting is striking because of the luminous quality of its colour and the humanity which can be seen in the pathetic face of the comedian.

46

*Jean-Honorè Fragonard
(1732-1806)*
The Bathers

Fragonard was the best-known and best-loved representative of French Rococo: a pupil of Boucher, he was greatly influenced by the style of Rubens in the sensual quality of his colour and the fullness of his forms. This canvas, perhaps painted in the period which followed the artist's first trip to Italy (from 1756 to 1761) and given to the Louvre in 1869, may have been done as a companion piece to the other work of the same subject, now part of a private American collection. The painting is a sort of hymn to life, sensuality and joy, but in forms

which have become almost immaterial and ethereal. But it is also the last breath, as it were, of a world which was unavoidably dying: with the changing times and new political sentiments, Fragonard's style could no longer be adapted to the tastes of the epoch, so much so that his death, in 1806, caused very little comment.

Camille Corot (1796-1875)
Woman with the Pearl

Painted in 1868 in the same pose as Leonardo's Mona Lisa, this splendid figure of a woman is something of a prototype among the portraits by Corot: the line is sure and confident, the figure is immersed in a calm light and there is a sense of peace and serenity, features which are typical of all the works by the great French painter, both his portraits and landscapes. It has been said of his art that he had the same way of looking at both men and nature, and indeed Corot approaches humanity and the material world with the same sincere feeling of respect and liking.

Jacques-Louis David (1748-1825)
Coronation of Napoleon I

With the coming of the French Revolution and the great changes which it brought in every field, artistic canons too were overturned. Rococo elegance was banished, and it was the Academy with its official tastes which now dictated the rules. The new era required its own interpreter and found him in Jacques-Louis David, who had been in sympathy with the revolutionaries and now became a fervent admirer of Napoleon, at whose side and under whose patronage he worked with great energy. After numerous sketches and drawings, David painted this enormous canvas with a surface of 580 square feet, representing the coronation of Napoleon which took place on 2 December 1804 in Nôtre-Dame. David worked on it from 1805 to 1807, with the help of his pupil Rouget as well, painting no less than 150 portraits, all of them vivid and solemn images. This work, which confirmed David definitively as the most important painter of the new Empire, displays an outstanding sense of equilibrium in its composition, besides solemnity and nobility of expression. One might say that each image and each figure (all historically recognisable) constitutes a portrait in itself because of the accuracy with which they are conceived and the coherency with which they are realised.

50

Théodore Géricault
(1791-1824)
The raft of the Medusa

Painted and exhibited in the Salon in 1819, this canvas takes its inspiration from a tragic historical event: the "Medusa" was a French frigate which in 1816 was carrying settlers to Senegal when it was shipwrecked during a storm because of the inexperience of the captain. Most of the 150 passengers died; the few who were saved clung to a life-raft and drifted aimlessly in the immensity of the ocean, torn by episodes of human violence and ferocity. Géricault relates the story with a crude realism, to which the violent contrasts of light and shade, learnt without doubt from Caravaggio, contribute. Géricault captured on canvas the moment in which the shipwreck victims sight a sail on the horizon, and a tremor of life and hope seems to run through the raft which has known horror and death. The whole composition, with its diagonal line. presents a mass of interlocked. disjointed bodies and dramatic, hallucinated expressions. Truly splendid, the figure of the old man holding up a now dead body, absorbed in his grief and desperation (which are the same grief and desperation of all the others), as solemn and dignified as a figure from Greek tragedy.

*Eugene Delacroix
(1798-1863)*
Death of Sardanapalos

Exhibited in the Salon in 1827-1828, this canvas was little appreciated because of its errors in perspective and above all because of the confusion which reigns in the foreground. The catologue of the Salon describes it thus: " .... the insurgents besiege him in his palace.... Reclining on a splendid bed, at the top of a huge pyre, Sardanapalos orders the eunuchs and servants of the royal palace to butcher the women and pages and even his favourite horses and dogs.... Aisheh, the Bactrian woman, because she cannot endure to be put to death by a slave, hangs herself from the columns which support the vault.... ". But Delacroix was not seeking order and precision of detail: his intention was to upset, disturb and exalt the mind of the viewer. The fascination of the Orient, the artist's long stay in Spain and Morocco and his celebration of the exotic and the mysterious have all left their mark on this canvas, as for example in the brilliant colours and in the gleam of the gold which blends with the red of the fabrics. Standing out above all is the sovereign, with his closed, indifferent expression, as he watches, unmoved by the massacre.

Eugene Delacroix (1798-1863)
Liberty leading the People

This painting, which is a sort of
political poster, is meant to celebrate the day of 28 July 1830,
when the people rose and dethroned
the Bourbon king. Alexandre
Dumas tell us that Delacroix's participation in the rebellious movements of July was mainly of a
sentimental nature. Despite this,
the painter, who had been a member
of the National Guard, took pleasure in portraying himself in the
figure on the left wearing the top-
hat. Although the painting is filled
with rhetoric, Delacroix's spirit is
fully involved in its execution: in
the outstretched figure of Liberty,
in the bold attitudes of the people
following her, contrasted with the
lifeless figures of the dead heaped
up in the foreground, in the heroic
poses of the people fighting for liberty, there is without doubt a
sense of full participation on the
part of the artist, which led Argan
to define this canvas as the first
political work of modern painting.

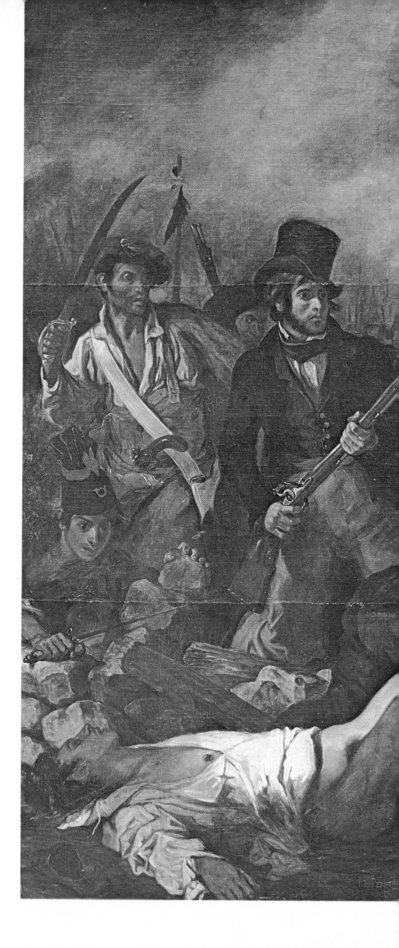

Frans Hals (1580-1666)
La Bohémienne

A Dutch painter, Hals had many
contacts with the northern followers
of Caravaggio, which led him to
depict in his canvasses members of
the lower classes, drinkers in tav-
erns, old drunken women. This
portrait, usually dated between 1628
and 1630, represents a gipsy woman,
dishevelled, smiling, with her corset
open at the breast. Hals' brush-
stroke is extremely rapid and intense, revealing the psychology of

the subject. It was part of the collection of de Marigny, brother of
Madame la Pompadour, then passed
into the Lacaze collection, from
which it was left by will to the
Louvre in 1869.

Rembrandt (1606-1669)
The Supper in Emmaus

Painted towards 1648 and acquired
by the Louvre in 1777, this Supper
in Emmaus is one of the works
which belong to the artist's period

of full maturity. Here, with extremely simple means, Rembrandt
attains to highly dramatic and mys-
tical effects. From the background
which is barely sketched in, the
face of Christ stands out powerfully,
illuminated by a supernatural light.
The whole work expresses the sacred
and solemn atmosphere of this supreme moment, in which the figures
are almost immobilised against the
the simple surroundings. The religious feeling emanated by this small
panel (27 × 26 in.) is really as-
tonishing.

ground, filtering laboriously through the fissures and clefts of the rocks until it illuminates the group in the foreground, with its rigorously pyramidal structure.

Leonardo da Vinci (1452-1519)
Mona Lisa (or The Gioconda)

Reams have been written about this small masterpiece by Leonardo, and the gentle woman who is its subject has been adapted in turn as an aesthetic, philosophical and advertising symbol, entering eventually into the irreverent parodies of the Dada and Surrealist artists. The history of the panel has been much discussed, although it remains in part uncertain. According to Vasari, the subject is a young Florentine woman, Monna (or Mona) Lisa, who in 1495 married the well-known figure, Francesco del Giocondo, and thus came to be known as " La Gioconda ". The work should probably be dated during Leonardo's second Florentine period, that is between 1503 and 1505. Leonardo himself loved the portrait, so much so that he always carried it with him until eventually in France it was sold to Francis I, either by Leonardo or by Melzi. From the beginning it was greatly admired and much copied, and it came to be considered the prototype of the Renaissance portrait. It became even more famous in 1911, when it was stolen from the Salon Carré in the Louvre, being rediscovered in a hotel in Florence two years later. It is difficult to discuss such a work briefly because of the complex stylistic motifs which are part of it. In the essay " On the perfect beauty of a woman ", by the 16th-century writer Firenzuola, we learn that the slight opening of the lips at the corners of the mouth was considered in that period a sign of elegance. Thus Mona Lisa has that slight smile which enters into the gentle, delicate atmosphere pervading the whole painting. To achieve this effect, Leonardo uses the *sfumato* technique, a gradual dissolving of the forms themselves, continuous interaction between light and shade and an uncertain sense of the time of day.

Leonardo da Vinci (1452-1519)
The Virgin of the Rocks

Begun, according to some critics, in Florence in 1483 but not completed until about 1490, this magnificent work corresponds to another version (most of which was painted by Ambrogio de Predis), now in the National Gallery in London.

Leonardo may have received the commission for the work from the Confraternity of San Francesco Grande in Milan; certainly, at any rate, the painting was at Fontainebleau in 1625, and this may permit us to deduce that it was part of the group of works by Leonardo acquired by Francis I. The light in this painting comes from the back-

Titian (1488-1576)
Woman at the mirror

This canvas by Titian is usually dated at 1515, that is in the period when the great Venetian painter was still to a large extent under the influence of Giorgione. In fact the warm golden nudity of the woman, the ample white corset opening in numerous folds on her breast and the mass of loose hair are typical of Giorgione. Some critics say that the woman portrayed here is Laura Dianti, the mistress of Alfonso d'Este, while others say that it is Titian's own mistress, but in any case she recurs in many other paintings by Titian.

Raphael (1483-1520)
Portrait of Baldassarre Castiglione

This canvas, dating from 1514-1515, portrays Baldassarre Castiglione, a friend of Raphael and the author of the celebrated " Cortegiano " (The Courtier). Raphael gives us a splendid interpretation of his subject, not only psychological but above all historical, portraying him with a noble, aristocratic espression. The work displays perfect harmony between linear and tonal values: the subject's form is tranquilly contained within the space created and the sober colours reach a perfect equilibrium of grey and gold tones. The pose, a three-quarter bust with the hands linked in front of the body and the figure majestically dressed in velvet and fur, recalls the pose in the portrait of Ginevra Benci and of the Mona Lisa. After leaving Italy, this canvas reached Amsterdam where it was sold at auction in 1639. It became part of the collection of Cardinal Mazzarino, and later entered the collection of Louis XIV.

Paolo Veronese (1528-1588)
The Marriage at Cana

Among the various Suppers which Paolo Veronese painted, this one in the Louvre is one of the finest. In this work, as in the others, the religious episode is no more than a pretext for the artist to describe a magnificent ceremonial occasion in the highly fashionable Venetian society of the 16th century. Within typically Palladian architectural surroundings, which allow the sunlight to enter freely, Veronese paints a crowd of more than 130 figures: princes, merchants, Turks, slaves, jesters, jugglers and dogs. He takes pleasure in describing in minute

detail the heavy damask materials, the highly worked silverware, the rich embroidery of the table-cloths. Veronese seems to have depicted among the many guests several important personalities of the Renaissance: Eleanor of Austria, the emperor Charles V, Vittoria Colonna, Mary of England and Suleiman. In the foreground, as if in a place of honour, the musicians are playing: Veronese painted himself at the violincello, Bassano playing the flute, Titian at the double-bass and Tintoretto at the viola. Painted for the refectory of the monastery of San Giorgio Maggiore in Venice, the work was begun in 1562 and completed barely a year later.

Pisanello (c. 1380-1455)
Portrait of a noblewoman of the Este family

There are many theories about the identity of the woman portrayed in this panel, painted in tempera by Pisanello. The amphora embroidered on her sleeve seems to indicate that she is a noblewoman of the Este family, possibly Ginevra, the wife of Sigismondo Malatesta, whereas the sprig of juniper on her corset and the red, white and green colours would identify her as a Gonzaga, Margherita, wife of Lionello d'Este. In any case, whatever is the name of this young woman, whose profile stands out against

the bush as if it were engraved, it is certain that the painting belongs to the artist's period of full maturity, that it was done towards 1436 or 1438. The flowers, butterflies and leaves which are behind the subject lose their reality to become splendid gems, looking as if they too were engraved on precious stones.

Andrea Mantegna (1431-1506)
St. Sebastian

Taken to a town in central France, Aigueperse, in 1481 when Chiara Gonzaga married Count Gilbert de Bourbon Montpensier, the canvas remained there until 1910. A monumental work, it was painted by Mantegna in robust blocks, showing that the artist had fully comprehended both the spirit of Roman architecture and the perspective vision of the Florentines. As can be seen, however, the viewpoint is lowered, so that both the saint and the architectural masses hang forwards towards the viewer. And it is precisely this fact which creates a sense of pathos and a heroic sentiment of the acceptance of pain and martyrdom, redeeming the scene from any hint of architectural coldness.

Paolo Uccello (1397-1475)
The Battle of San Romano

Paolo Uccello painted three panels (now divided between the Louvre, the National Gallery in London and the Uffizi in Florence) depicting the three crucial moments in the battle which took place in June 1432 at San Romano between the Florentines, under the command of Niccolò Mauruzi da Tolentino, and the Sienese, led by Bernardino della Ciarda. In this panel in the Louvre, Uccello painted one of the decisive developments in the battle, the intervention of Micheletto da Cotignola on the side of the Florentines. The military captain is shown in the centre of the whole composition, as the horses paw the ground waiting for the attack. The lances of the soldiers stand out above the geometric suits of armour and elaborate helmets and crests. The panel (this is the best preserved of the three, in that it still retains the silver-plating on the armour) was painted along with the other two between 1451 and 1457 for the Medici Palace. The three are mentioned as still being together in an inventory of the collections of Lorenzo the Magnificent done in 1498; later the Medici Palace was acquired by the Riccardi family, and the panels were transferred to the Palazzo Vecchio where they remained until the second half of the 18th century. This panel reached the Louvre in 1863 by way of the Campana collection.

CAROLVS·I
MAGNÆ
ANNÆ

Antony van Dyck (1599-1641)
Portrait of Charles I

A pupil and helper of Rubens, Anthony van Dyck came from the same background as his master but broke away at an early stage to establish his own, highly personal style. Summoned to England by Charles I, he became the official painter of the royal court and was also knighted. During his stay there (which lasted from 1632 to 1641), he did many portraits of the monarch, but this work, painted in about 1635, is the most celebrated and the finest of them. Here Charles I is portrayed as a typical English gentleman after his return from the hunt. The brilliant, almost shrill colours of Ru-

bens are attenuated into softer, more delicate tones: the strong passions of his master have become in the pupil a sort of absorbed psychological introspection. The portraits of van Dyck established a tradition in England which was to put down deep roots and later to be enriched by numerous artists.

Peter Paul Rubens (1577-1640)
La Kermesse

Perhaps no other artist succeeded so brilliantly as Rubens in combining the colour technique of the Venetians with the Flemish tradition. With him the Baroque school

had its greatest triumph: a triumph of colour, of the exaltation of life, an impetus of joy. This highly animated composition belongs to the final period of Rubens' activity, that is to about 1635 or 1638. The recollection of the Kermesses, the dances in the fields, and the open-air feasts painted by Breughel the Elder can certainly be felt: like his predecessor, he liked to create a figure rotating in space and transmitting this movement to the figures beside it and thence throughout the whole group. The entire scene thus becomes a series of whirling couples clutching each other, figures which tend to lose their human identity and be transformed into spirals of dynamic movement and colour.

Hans Memling (c. 1433-1494)
Portrait of an Old Woman

This small painting on panel was originally a companion piece to the Portrait of an Old Man (now in the Staatliche Museen in Berlin), and in fact they were sold at auction together by the collector Meazza in Milan on 15 April 1884. Later they were separated and this Portrait of an Old Woman passed through the hands of various private collectors until it was finally acquired by the Louvre in 1908. Apparently painted towards 1470 or 1475, it shows the woman in a half-bust figure, closed geometrically in her dress and placed in front of a landscape according to the Flemish tradition, followed previously by van der Weyden.

Quentin Metsys (1465-1530)
The banker and his wife

This panel has the inscription " Quinten matsyss schilder, 1514 ": it is thus a signed work by Quinten Metsys, an important Flemish artist

who belonged to the transition between the Middle Ages and the Renaissance and who painted altarpieces as well as non-religious subjects. In Metsys' work, genre painting assumed an importance which until then only works of a religious nature had had. The artist's moralistic or satirical intentions are evident, in this panel as elsewhere in his work. Here he has carefully described the surroundings in the most minute detail and painted the banker as he is weighing coins on a scale. His wife, who has been occupied up until now reading a sacred book, looks up, visibly attracted by the glitter of the gold. The illuminated page of the book thus remains open, while a round mirror (reflecting a window and the landscape outside) stand as a symbol of vanity.

François Clouet (mentioned 1536-1572)
Portrait of Elizabeth of Austria

Son of the other great painter, Jean Clouet, François succeeded his father as court painter in 1540. In this portrait, painted with a sure mastery of line and a particularly delicate use of colours, the artist depicted the daughter of the Austrian emperor, Maximilian, who on 27 November 1570 married the king of France, Charles IX.

Francisco Goya (1746-1828)
The Countess of Carpio

At almost the same time in which the passionate, complex mind of Goya was creating the Caprices, the painter was still able to paint serene and delicate works like this portrait of " Dona Rita de Barrenechea, Marquesa de la Solana y Condesa del Carpio ", done between 1794 and 1795. Goya's famous portraits, painted for members of the court circle, represent the other side of his art, a far more relaxed side which is not concerned with the anguish and disasters which war and the hypocrisy and evil of man bring about. Behind the Countess, Goya creates an empty space, which throws into relief the sumptuous black velvet of her long dress,

the fine white lace of her mantilla and the large pink rose, realised with a few skilful touches of light.

Diego Velasquez (1599-1660)
The Infante Marguerite

Velasquez painted many portraits of the Infante Marguerite, daughter of Philip IV and of Marianna of Austria. This canvas, done in about 1653, may have been one of the royal portraits which the king sent to his sister Anna, Queen of France. The painting belongs to the finest, most mature period of Velasquez' artistic activity at the court of Spain: his colour has reached its warmest tones, his chromatic relations are at their most exact, while the luminous quality which touches the face of the child is not all aggressive, but combines smoothly and precisely with the golden yellow mass of her hair. In a job of restoration done in 1659, the words at the top of the painting, " LINFANTE MARGUERITE ", which had been added later, were removed.

Esteban Murillo (1618-1682)
Young Beggar

Murillo, unlike other famous Spanish painters who were among his predecessors, kept his distance both from the luxuries of the court and from their gloomy and obsessive mysticism. His faith has a serene quality, untouched by anguish and doubt, while at the same time his scenes of the daily life of the common people are never dramatic or unpleasant. Even in conditions of poverty, in fact, Murillo seeks the most beautiful and delicate aspects, far from the dramatic effects created by the violent contrast between light and shade typical of Caravaggio. Thus this young beggar, despite the rags and tatters of his clothes, is a finely drawn, pathetic figure: he inspires in the viewer, not repulsion, but a tender sense of compassion. The painting, previously in Cordova, was later acquired by the royal palace of Madrid. It is not known how it came into France, but once there it became the property of Louis XVI.

Jean-Auguste Ingres (1780-1867)
The Turkish Bath

This famous painting by Ingres, the inspiration for which certainly came from the description of a harem in the Letters of Lady Montague, was originally framed and was the property of Prince Napoleon. On the insistence of his wife, who considered the picture unbecoming because of the large number of nudes which it contained, Napoleon in April 1860 returned the work to Ingres who kept it in his studio until 1863, working on it continually and modifying it in various ways, one of which was to change it into a tondo. The Turkish ambassador in Paris, Khalil Bey, bought it for 20,000 francs, and later it came into the hands of Prince de Broglie, finally reaching the Louvre in 1911. The painting can be considered a synthesis of all the experiences which Ingres had begun sixty years before: the drawing technique has become extremely slender and sinuous, the colour limpid, almost dazzling. A continuous line unites all the bodies to each other, immersed as they are in their sensual surroundings with a heavy atmosphere of Oriental perfumes. The nude bodies of the women, although they are highly abstract, are touched by an emotional tremor which renders them extremely natural.

Jean-Baptiste Chardin (1699-1779)
Still-life with Pipe

Under the influence of Enlightenment culture, the little things and lesser experiences of daily life finally took over from the supernatural myths which until then had dominated artistic interests. Chardin took his place in this tradition and was at his most outstanding in the depiction of still-lifes and of simple, commonplace objects. This painting, dated at about 1760 or 1763, is a sober, essential work. The objects are placed according to a rigid criterion, each one suspended in its own precisely determined space, ideally linked to each other, though at the same time each one has its own valid reality.

Gustave Courbet (1819-1877)
Burial at Ornans

With Gustave Courbet, the real figures of everyday life, the peasants, the poor and the lower middle class, make their entry into art. Considered the main exponent of the French Realist school, Courbet here painted a simple scene from the village where he was born, Ormans, among the Jural mountains. The composition of the work is of great simplicity, with no hint of rhetoric (to which the subject could easily have lent itself), and it is rightly considered as marking the birth of Realism: its protagonist is the humble population of Ornans, painted with dark, gloomy colours, almost life-size and imbued with nobility and dignity.

Annibale Carracci (1560-1609)
The Hunt and Fishing

Both given to Louis XIV in 1665 by the Roman prince Camillo Pamphili, the two canvasses reflect a happy moment in the art of Annibale Carracci who, together with his brother Agostino and cousin Ludovico, had founded in Bologna in 1585 a school of fine arts called the Accademia degli Incamminati, the aim of which was to supersede the then empty formulas of Mannerism and seek a more direct contact with nature. The dating of the works can be tentatively put at around 1585, that is, in the artist's first period at Bologna when the reminiscences of Correggio are most felt in his work. His description of the landscape is serene and tranquil, and the men are captured in fresh, natural and spontaneous attitudes.

PLACE VENDÔME

Another masterpiece by Jules Hardouin-Mansart (who had already designed Place des Victoires), this square received its name from from the fact that the Duke of Vendôme had his residence here. It was created between 1687 and 1720 to surround an equestrian statue by Girardon dedicated to Louis XIV, later destroyed, like so many others, during the Revolution. A perfect example of stylistic simplicity and austerity, it is octagonal in form and surrounded by buildings which have large arches on the lower floor; on the foreparts of the buildings are skilfully distributed pediments and they are crowned, on the roofs, by numerous dormer-windows, so typical that some have thought to see in this square a synthesis of the spirit and style of Paris. There are important buildings here today: the famous Hôtel Ritz at number 15, the house where Chopin died in 1849 at number 12 and the residence of Eugenia de Montijo, future wife of Napoleon III. In the centre of the square stands the famous column erected by Gondouin and Lepère between 1806 and 1810 in honour of Napoleon I. Inspired by the Column of Trajan in Rome, it is 145 feet high and around the shaft is a spiral series of bas-reliefs, cast from the 1200 canons captured at Austerlitz, in which the sculptor Bergeret sought to hand down to posterity the Napoleonic exploits. On the top of the column, Antoine-Denise Chaudet erected a statue of the emperor which was destroyed in 1814 and replaced by that of Henry IV. Later, in 1863, a statue of Napoleon was put back in place, but eight years later again, at the time of the Commune (when the voice of the great painter Gustave Courbet had a decisive say), the statue was taken down once more, only to be replaced once and for all by another replica of Napoleon three years afterwards.

OPÉRA

The largest theatre for lyric opera in the world (in fact its surface area covers nearly 120,000 square feet, it can accommodate more than 2000 people and there is room on its stage for no less than 450 performers), it is also perhaps the most interesting building from the era of Napoleon III. Designed by Garnier and built between 1862 and 1875, its façade displays that profusion of decorative elements which was typical of the era. An ample stairway leads up to the first of the two orders into which the façade is divided, with its large arches and robust pillars, in front of which are numerous marble groups of sculpture. At the second pillar on the right can be seen what is considered the masterpiece of Jean-Baptiste Carpeaux, "The Dance" (the original is now in the Louvre). The second order of the façade consists of tall double columns which frame large windows; above is an attic, with exuberant decoration, and above this again the flattened cupola. The interior is just as highly decorated as the façade: the monumental stairway is enriched by marbles, the vault is decorated with paintings by Isidore Pils and the hall has a large painting by Chagall done in 1966.

LA MADELEINE

A Greek temple in the middle of Paris, this is certainly a rather extraordinary structure. It was Napoleon who wanted to erect a monument in honour of the Great Army, built along the lines of the Maison Carrée at Nîmes. To do so, he had a previous structure, which was not yet complete, totally demolished, and work was resumed from scratch in 1806, under the direction of the architect Vignon. In 1814 it became a church dedicated to St. Mary Magdalene, standing in the centre of the square of the same name. It has the form and structure of a classical Greek temple: a high base with a large stairway in front, a colonnade with with 52 Corinthian columns 65 feet high running round the outside of the structure and a pediment with a large frieze sculpted by Lemaire in 1834 and representing the Last Judgment. The interior is aisleless, and it has a vestibule, in which are two sculptural groups by Pradier and Rude, and a semicircular apse. Above the high altar is a work by an Italian artist, the Assumption of Mary Magdalene by Marocchetti. As one leaves the building, one's gaze takes in the whole length of the Rue Royale, as far as the obelisk in Place de la Concorde and the Palais Bourbon.

PALAIS BOURBON

This building bears the signature of no less than four famous architects: Giardini began it in 1722, Lassurance continued its construction, and Aubert and Gabriel completed it in 1728. It was originally built for the daughter of Louis XIV, the Duchess of Bourbon, who gave her name to the building. In 1764 it became the property of the Condé princes, who had it extended to its present dimensions, an imposing and noble structure looking over the square of the same name. Between 1803 and 1807 Napoleon had Poyet construct the façade, facing towards the Seine and harmonising with the façade of the Madeleine church opposite it in the distance, at the end of Rue Royale. The portico of the façade has an allegorical pediment, sculpted by Cortot in 1842. Other allegorical bas-reliefs on the wings are the work of Rude and Pradier. The interior has a wealth of works of art: suffice to say that Delacroix between 1838 and 1845 decorated its library with the History of Civilisation and in the same room are busts of Diderot and Voltaire sculpted by Houdon.

PLACE DE LA CONCORDE

Created between 1757 and 1779 to a design by Jacques-Ange Gabriel on land donated by the king in 1743, the square was originally dedicated to Louis XV and there was an equestrian statue of the king, a work by Bouchardon and Pigalle, in the centre, pulled down during the French Revolution. In the Revolution, this became the site of the guillotine, under whose blade so many great figures of the time lost their heads: from the king, Louis XVI, and his queen, Marie Antoinette, to Madame Roland and Robespierre. The square became Place de la Concorde in 1795, and its present-day appearance dates from work supervised by the architect Hittorf between 1836 and 1840. In the centre of the square today stands the Egyptian obelisk from the temple of Luxor, donated to Louis Philippe in 1831 by Mehmet-Alì. Erected in 1836, it is 75 feet high and covered with hieroglyphics which illustrate the glorious deeds of the pharaoh

Ramses II. Eight statues, symbolising the main cities of France, stand at the corners of the square. To the north of the square, on either side of Rue Royale, are the colonnaded buildings (these too designed by Gabriel) containing the Ministry of the Navy and the Hôtel Crillon.

PLACE DE LA CONCORDE
Fountain

Built on the model of the fountains in Piazza S. Pietro in Rome, these two fountains at the sides of the obelisk were erected by Hittorf between 1836 and 1846; they have

several basins and the statues adorning them represent fluvial allegories. There are perhaps few squares in the world with the magic atmosphere of enchantment present at every hour of the day in this square. Indeed at night, under the light of the street-lamps, its atmosphere becomes unreal, almost fable-like.

GRAND PALAIS

The World Fair held in Paris in 1900 was an important step in the history of the city's art and architecture. For the occasion, monuments and works of art were created in a modern style which was almost too eclectic and bombastic. As a reflection of this taste, the two adjacent buildings called the Petit Palais and the Grand Palais were erected, both of huge dimensions and characterised by their ample colonnades, friezes and sculptural compositions. The Grand Palais, built by Deglane and Louvet, has a façade with Ionic columns, 787 feet long and 65 feet high. Today important artistic events take place here, including exhibitions of painting, whereas previously its vast area served for fairs, motor shows and similar exhibitions. Part of it is permanently occupied by the Palais de la Découverte (Discovery), where the latest conquests of science and steps in man's progress are celebrated.

GRAND PALAIS - Chariot

The corners of the Grand Palais are crowned by enormous chariots, like the one shown here, which give very much the impression that they want to hurl themselves from the points where they stand into the surrounding space. The inside of the Grand Palais has a huge room covered by a flattened cupola 141 feet high.

PONT ALEXANDRE III

One of Paris's many bridges, this has a single metal span 350 feet long and 130 feet wide joining the Esplanade des Invalides to the Champs-Elysées. Built between 1896 and 1900, it is named after the czar Alexander III whose son, Nicholas II, performed its inauguration. In fact the bridge was built to celebrate the creation of the alliance between the Russians and the French. Garlands of flowers, lamps held up by cherubs and allegorical figures of marine deities make up the decorative motifs of the bridge. On the two pilons on the right bank are representations of medieval France and modern France, while on the left-bank pilons are statues representing Renaissance France and the France of the time of Louis XIV. Allegorical representations of the Seine and the Neva, symbols again of France and Russia, decorate the pilons at the entries to the bridge.

JEU DE PAUME MUSEUM

The Jeu de Paume Museum, the Museum of French Impressionism, owes its name to Napoleon III, who had the Feuillants terrace in the Tuileries adapted for the game of " paume ", an earlier form of tennis. This game was substituted in the first years of the 20th century by the introduction of lawn-tennis, but the name Jeu de Paume remained, although the area was now converted to accommodate exhibitions of paintings. The first of these, in 1909, was an exhibition of portraits of women by the French and English schools of the 19th century.

In 1924, Léonce Benedite thought of transferring here the collection of modern painting by foreigners in the Museum of Luxembourg, of which he was the curator. Later, in 1947, the chief curator of the department of painting, René Huyghe, reserved it exclusively for Impressionist works. Today it contains a vast synthesis, the only one of its kind in the world, of the experiments and of the outstanding contributions which Impressionism made to art.

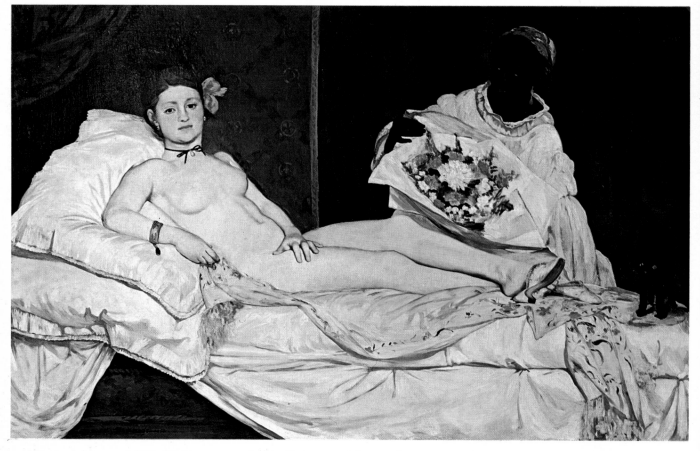

Edouard Manet (1832-1883)
Olympia

" What is this odalisque with her yellow belly? " exclaimed a critic confronted with Manet's Olympia at the 1865 Salon. The picture, painted in 1863, scandalised the public and the official critics: it was inconceivable at the time for a female nude to be painted with a technique which was so irreverent towards the then accepted artistic canons. And Manet indeed makes a total break with tradition: he destroys volume and abolishes all the intermediate colour tones and the half-tints, relying only on a free association of colour tones. The result is thus a very flat style of painting, in which every element is simplified to the point of pure abstraction. Manet used this revolutionary technique, however, within a classical and traditional framework, in that he took his inspiration for the nude Olympia from Goya and, even more so, from Titian's Venus of Urbino.

Edouard Manet (1832-1883)
The Balcony

This painting was not acquired by the museum until 1929, having remained until then in the artist's studio, alongside his Olympia. In fact, the same polemics and criticism provoked previously by the Olympia were revived for this work, due to its violent contrasts, absence of chiaroscuro and flat forms, detached from the background. The master from whom Manet took his inspiration this time was Goya, with his " Majas al balcone ". The white dresses of the figures stand out in the blinding light of day as they look down from the balcony at something taking place in the street below.

Camille Pissarro (1830-1903)
Red Roofs

Within the panorama of the Impressionist school, Camille Pissarro has his own independent personality, though it was without doubt derived from the contacts which he had first with Monet and later, more importantly, with Cézanne. Manet stayed with Cézanne at Pontoise in 1877, and during this period of work together Pissarro gave much to Cézanne and at the same time received much from him. This work, dating from the period with Cézanne, gives us the exact impression of an autumn landscape, when the trees are bare and the dry shrubs and the ground are strewn with a mantle of red and golden leaves. A glimpse can be had, between the twisted branches, of the sharp red roofs of a small village, the structure of which remains solid and compact despite the restless glimmerings of light and the rapid touches of the painter's brush.

Henri Toulouse-Lautrec (1864-1901)
The Clownesse Cha-U-Kao

Linked to no particular school or artistic movement, Henri Toulouse-Lautrec remains, among the most important exponents of Impressionism, the artist who was least touched by the polemics which raged in the cafés and studios of Paris during those years, so important for the formation of modern art. Concealing his deformed figure in the smoky, noise-filled night spots of Montmartre, he sat at a table all night, rapidly sketching on paper not only the physical but also the psychological aspects of the characters who alternated on the stage: the elegant and refined Jean Avril; la Goulue, the washerwoman who became the prima ballerina at the Moulin Rouge; the celebrated Valentin le Désossé ("the Boneless"); and the female clown, Cha-U-Kao, a pathetic personality from this world of poor players who, even in her gaudy costume, reveals a gentle humanity and a sad sense of resignation.

Georges Seurat (1859-1891)
The Circus

Seurat, one of the major representatives of Post-Impressionism, decided to apply to his art the results which the scientific research of the period had achieved in the fields of optics and physics. Conscious of the fact that colours near each other in the spectrum influence each other (a law formulated by Chevreul), Seurat created so-called Divisionism or " Pointillisme ", a technique in which he covered the surface of the canvas with dots of colour, achieving effects of great lightness and luminosity. This painting, dating from 1890, was exhibited at the Salon des Indépendants the following year: as it happened, Seurat died suddenly in March of the same year, during the exhibition, and the painting, which was uncompleted, remained at the stage of a coloured drawing.

Paul Cézanne (1839-1906)
Still-life with Onions

Paul Cézanne, one of the creators of modern art, was called the " solidifier of Impressionism ". And indeed he does not draw his picture before painting it: instead, he creates space and depth of perspective by means of planes of colour, which are freely associated and at the same time contrasted and compared. The facets which are thus produced create not just one but many perspectives, and in this way volume comes once again to dominate the composition, no longer a product of the line but rather of the colour itself. This painting, in its simplicity and delicate tonal harmony, is a typical work and thus ideal for an understanding of Cézanne's art.

Paul Gauguin (1848-1903)
Tahitian women

Gauguin's art has all the appearance of a flight from civilisation, of a search for new ways of life, more primitive, more real and more sincere. His break away from a solid middle-class world, abandoning family, children and job, his refusal to accept easy glory and easy gain are the best-known aspects of Gauguin's fascinating life and personality. This picture, also known as " Two women on the beach ", was painted in 1891, shortly after Gauguin's arrival in Tahiti. During his first stay there (he was to leave in 1893, only to return in 1895 and remain until his death), Gauguin discovered primitive art, with its flat forms and the violent colours belonging to an untamed nature. And then, with absolute sincerity, he transferred them onto canvas.

Vincent Van Gogh (1853-1890)
The Church at Auvers

A brief description of the art of Van Gogh is virtually impossible: the artist's personality is far too complex and out of the ordinary to be summed up in a few lines. It may suffice in part, however, to " read " this painting, done at Auvers-sur-Oise in June 1890 and thus belonging to the last period of the artist's life, his most troubled and unhappy period. In fact Van Gogh had taken refuge in this tiny and ancient village, where Cézanne and Pissarro had previously stayed, in May of the same year, after leaving the psychiatric hospital of Saint-Rémy. Here at Auvers he had brief periods of calm and illusory serenity, followed by crises of anguish and madness. He was to write to his sister Wil: " .... I have painted a large picture of the village church, in which the structure seems violet against the deep blue sky, a pure cobalt; the stained-glass windows appear as ultramarine blue marks; the roof is violet and in part orange.... ". What Van Gogh does not write, because he cannot write it, is the fact that a violent, almost mad sense of drama emerges from the dense, contorted brush-strokes, from the colour applied heavily, in thick layers. In Van Gogh, the sky is never a serene, clear sky, but always appears as if agitated by obscure celestial forces; the long lances of the cypress trees seem to be twisting flames and the sun is always ready to explode. In short, the brush-stroke reveals the artist's state of mind. And since Van Gogh had a tragic vision of life, he filled both men and objects with violence and desperation, distorting and transforming everything.

CHAMPS-ÉLYSÉES

Originally this vast area lying to the west of Place de la Concorde was swamp land. After its reclamation, le Nôtre in 1667 designed the wide avenue called Grand-Cours (it became the Champs-Elysées in 1709), reaching from the Tuileries as far as Place dell'Etoile, today called Place de Gaulle. At the beginning of the avenue are the horses of Marly, a work by Guillaume Coustou; from this point as far as the Ronde Point of the Champs-Elysées the avenue is flanked by a park. At the time of the Second Empire, this became the most fashionable meeting-place and upper-class residential area in all Paris. Today it may no longer have its one-time aristocratic character. but it has lost nothing of its beauty and elegance: luxurious shops, theatres, famous restaurants and important airline offices line its wide footpaths, which are always full of Parisians, tourists and a cosmopolitan throng.

ARCH
OF TRIUMPH

At the end of the Champs-Elysées, at the top of the Chaillot hill, is the large Place de Gaulle; radiating outwards from this square are no less than twelve main arteries. Isolated in the centre stands the powerful and imposing Arch of Triumph, begun by Chalgrin in 1806 under Napoleon, who ordered it as a memorial to the Great Army. Completed in 1836, it has a single barrel-vault and actually exceeds in size the Arch of Constantine in Rome: in fact it is 164 feet high and 147 feet wide. The faces of the arch have huge bas-reliefs, of which the best known and finest piece is that on the right, on the part of the arch facing the Champs-Elysées, depicting the departure of the volunteers in 1792 and called the " Marseillaise ". The principal vic-tories of Napoleon are celebrated in the other bas-reliefs higher up, while the shields sculpted in the top section bear the names of the great battles. Under the arch the Tomb of the Unknown Soldier was placed in 1920 and its eternal flame is tended every evening. There is a history of the monument in a small museum inside the arch, where one can read the names of no less than 558 generals, some of them underlined because they died on the battlefield.

EIFFEL TOWER

If the symbol of Rome is the Colosseum, then Paris's symbol is without doubt the Eiffel Tower: both are monuments unique in planning and construction, both stir admiration by their extraordinary dimensions, and both bear witness to man's inborn will to build something capable of demonstrating the measure of his genius. The tower was erected on the occasion of the World Fair in 1889. These were the years of the Industrial Revolution, of progress and of scientific conquests. The attempt was made to adapt every art to the new direction which life had taken and to make every human activity correspond to the new sensibility created by the rapidly changing times. Architecture also underwent radical changes: glass, iron and steel were the new construction materials, the most suitable ones to make buildings lighter, more dynamic and more modern. The engineer, in short, had taken the place of the architect. And indeed it was an engineer, Gustave Eiffel, who designed — not on paper but on the surface of the sky itself — these extraordinary lines of metal, which soar above the Parisian skyline and seem to triumph over all the older monuments of the city. While the older buildings symbolise the past, the Eiffel Tower anticipates the future and the conquests which man will achieve.

Altogether 1050 feet high, the Eiffel Tower is an extremely light, interlaced structure in which no less than 15,000 pieces of metal are welded together. Its extraordinary weight of 7000 tons rests on four enormous pilons with cement bases. It has three floors: the first at 187 feet, the second at 377 feet and the third at 899 feet. On each of the floors there are bars and restaurants, allowing the tourist to pause there and enjoy the unique panoramic view: at times, on days when the visibility is perfect, one can see almost 45 miles. Beneath the Eiffel Tower is the green area of the Champs-de-Mars, a military field at one time but later transformed into a garden. During the Ancien Régime and during the Revolution many festivals were held here, including the Festival of the Supreme Being, introduced by Robespierre and celebrated on 8 June 1794. Then, in modern times, the vast area has been used for numerous World Fairs. Today the garden, whose design was supervised by Formigé between 1908 and 1928, is divided by wide avenues and scattered with flower gardens and small watercourses.

PALAIS DE CHAILLOT

Another World Fair, the one held in 1937, was the occasion for which this building was constructed. It was designed by the architects Boileau, Carlu and Azéma on the site of a previous building, the Trocadéro. The Palais de Chaillot has a central terrace with statues of gilded bronze, uniting two enormous pavilions which stretch out into two wings, as if in a long, curving embrace. From here a splendid complex of terraces, stairways and gardens slopes down to the Seine, a triumph of greenery made even more pleasant by the sounds of waterfalls and the jets of fountains. The two pavilions, on the front of which are inscribed verses by the poet Valéry, today contain the Museum of French Monuments (an important collection of medieval works), the Museum of the Navy (in which is a model of the ship " La Belle Poule " which brought back Napoleon's remains from St. Helena) and the Museum of Man, with its wealth of anthropological collections and documentation of the human race.

MILITARY SCHOOL

This building, which stands at the south end of the Champs-de-Mars, was constructed as a result of the initiative of the financier Pâris-Duverney and of Madame Pompadour, both of whom wanted young men of the poorer classes to be able to take up military careers. Jacques-Ange Gabriel was the architect of the building, erected between 1751 and 1773 in a sober style characterised by its harmonious lines. The façade has two orders of windows,

and in the centre is a pavilion with columns which support the pediment, decorated with statues and covered by a cupola. On the back, from Place de Fontenoy, one can see the elegant Courtyard of Honour with its portico of twin Doric columns and a façade formed by three pavilions linked by two rows of columns. The building still serves as a military school today. In 1784 Napoleon Bonaparte entered it as a pupil, to leave the following year with the rank of second lieutenant in the artillery.

RODIN MUSEUM

Auguste Rodin (1840-1917)
The Citizens of Calais and the Thinker

The Rodin Museum, which contains about 500 works by the celebrated sculptor, is situated in the Hôtel Biron in Rue de Varenne, a building constructed by Gabriel and Aubert which later became the property of Marshall de Biron. Educated in Paris during the years of Impressionism, Auguste Rodin brought to his sculpture all the expressive vigour and emotional power of that school. The Citizens of Calais is a profound psychological study of six different figures, with effects of light and shade

which only Impressionism could have taught the artist.

The Thinker, on the other hand, with its closed air of melancholy and reserve and massive sense of oppression, has the appearance of a figure derived from Michelangelo. This sculpture, unlike others which did not meet with great success either with the critics or with the public, was much appreciated and became so popular that Rodin himself made several copies of it.

LES INVALIDES

Stretching between Place Vauban and the Esplanade des Invalides, this vast complex of buildings includes the Hôtel des Invalides, the Dôme and the church of St. Louis. The whole construction, ordered by Louis XIV and entrusted to Libéral Bruant in 1671, was designed as a refuge for old and invalid soldiers who were then often forced to beg for a living. Completed in 1676, it later saw the addition of the church of St. Louis and the Dôme, designed by J. Harduoin-Mansart. The vast square of the Esplanade, 520 yards long and 270 yards wide, designed between 1704 and 1720, creates the right surroundings for the Hôtel des Invalides. In the garden in front of the Hôtel are a line of bronze cannon from the 17th and 18th centuries, eighteen pieces which belong to the " triumphal battery " and are fired only on important occasions, and at the sides of the entrance are two German tanks captured in 1944. The severe and dignified façade, 643 feet long, has four orders of windows and a majestic portal in the centre, surmounted by a relief representing Louis XIV with Prudence and Justice at his sides. Entering the courtyard, one can see the regular forms of the four sides with their two storeys of arcades. The pavilion at the end thus becomes the façade of the church of St. Louis. In the centre is the statue of Napoleon by Seurre, which was previously on top of the column in Place Vendôme. Worth seeing inside the church of St. Louis-des-Invalides is the Chapel of Napoleon, in which is kept the hearse in which the remains of the emperor were taken to St. Helena for burial and the sarcophagus in which Napoleon's body was brought back to France in 1840.

on the following page

DÔME DES INVALIDES

Considered one of the masterpieces of the architect Hardouin-Mansart, it was erected between 1679 and 1706. Pure forms and a classical, sober style are the characteristics of this building, with its square plan and two orders. The façade

is a work of elegance and symmetry: above the two orders of columns surmounted by a pediment is the solid mass of the drum with its twin columns, from which, after a sober series of corbels, the slim cupola springs with its decorations of flower garlands and other floral motifs. The gilded leaves with which the top is decorated shine in the sunlight, and the structure is terminated by a small lantern with spire 350 feet above ground level. The interior, in the form of a Greek cross, reflects the simplicity characteristic of the exterior. In the pendentives of the dome Charles de la Fosse painted the four Evangelists, while in the centre he depicted the figure of St. Louis offering Christ the sword with which he has defeated the infidels. Directly under the dome is the entrance to the crypt which contains the tomb of Napoleon. Indeed, this church could be said to be a shrine to the memory of Napoleon. Here too are tombs of members of the emperor's family, as well as those of other great Frenchmen. In the chapels on the right are the tombs of Napoleon's brother, Joseph Bonaparte, and of the two marshals Vauban and Foch. The emperor's other brother, Jérôme, is buried in the first chapel on the left, and his tomb is followed by those of Turenne and Lyautey.

TOMB OF NAPOLEON I

Napoleon Bonaparte died on 5 May 1821 on St. Helena, but not until seven years later were the French able to obtain permission from England to bring back the remains of their emperor to his own country. Louis Philippe sent his son, the prince of Joinville, to St. Helena to supervise the exhumation of the emperor's body. The re-entry into France was the last triumphal voyage of the Frenchman best loved by his people, most venerated by his soldiers and most feared by his enemies. In September 1840 a French ship carried the body of Napoleon to Le Havre, then slowly made the entire trip up the Seine as far as Paris. On 15 September, in a snow storm, almost the entire city attended the funeral of the emperor, whose body moved in a slow procession along the great boulevards, passing under the Arch of Triumph and descending the Champs-Elysées to come to rest here in the Dôme des Invalides and thus end at last Napoleon's long exile. Like those of an Egyptian pharaoh, the remains were contained in six coffins: the first of tin, the second of mahogany, the third and fourth of lead, the fifth of ebony and the sixth of oak. These were then placed in the huge sarcophagus of red granite, in the crypt specially planned for the purpose by the great architect Visconti. Here

12 enormous Victories, the work of Pradier, keep a vigil over the emperor, as if to symbolise the whole French people, finally reunited with their great hero. And is if to unite him after death with one from whom he had been divided during his life, next to the tomb was placed the tomb of Napoleon's son, the King of Rome, known romantically as l'Aiglon (the " Eaglet ").

PALAIS DU LUXEMBOURG

On the death of Henry IV, his queen, Maria de' Medici, who apparently did not feel at home in the Louvre, preferred to live in a

place which in some way reminded her of Florence, the city from which she came. Thus in 1612 she acquired this mansion from the duke François de Luxembourg, together with a considerable expanse of ground, and in 1615 she commissioned Salomon de Brosse to build a palace as near as possible in style and materials to the Florentine palaces which she had left to come to France. And in fact both the rusticated stonework and the large columns and rings are much more reminiscent of the Palazzo Pitti in Florence that of any other Parisian building. The façade consists of a pavilion with two orders covered by a cupola and with two pavilions at the sides, united to the central unit by galleries. When the Revolution broke out, the palace was taken from the royal family and transformed into a state prison.

On 4 November 1795, the first Directory installed itself here, and later Napoleon decided that it would be the seat of the Senate. Inside the palace are works by Eugène Delacroix and by Jordaens.

JARDIN DU LUXEMBOURG

Medici Fountain

Perhaps one of the most pleasant and typical things about Paris, this city with so many different aspects, is that beside roads crowded with traffic, people and noise there are hidden angles of greenery and silence, oases of peace where time slows to a stop. One of these places which calm the spirit is the Jardin du Luxembourg, a huge public park which, because it is near the Latin Quarter, is animated every day by young people and students. Among the trees throughout its vast are there are fountains, groups of statues and even playing fields. A fine series of statues are those depicting the queens of France and other illustrious woman along the terraces of the park. At the end of a canal on the eastern side of the Palais du Luxembourg, in a lush green setting, is the splendid Medici Fountain, attributed to Salomon de Brosse. In the central niche, Polyphemus is depicted as he surprises Galatea with the shepherd Acis, a work done by Ottin in 1863, while on the back is a bas-relief by Valois dating from 1806 and depicting Leda and the Swan.

FOUNTAIN OF THE OBSERVATORY

If one leaves the Jardin du Luxembourg going in the direction of the Observatory, one passes along the magnificent tree-lined Avenue de l'Observatoire. Here, in its green setting, is the celebrated fountain, also known as the " Fountain of the Four Corners of the Earth ". A work done by Davioud in 1875, it has the famous group of girls who symbolise the four corners of the earth, unusually beautiful and graceful figures sculpted by Carpeaux.

◄ ST. ETIENNE DU MONT

This church, one of the most remarkable in Paris both for its façade and for the interior, stands in the city's most picturesque zone, the Latin Quarter. From as early as the 13th century the University of Paris was established here, a university which immediately became famous throughout the world of Western culture because of the names of the great masters who gave lessons there: St. Bonaventura and St. Thomas Aquinas, to name only the most important. In this area, then, the original St. Etienne du Mont was built; it was begun in 1492 but completed only in 1622 with the construction of the façade. It is impossible not to be struck by the originality of this church.

In fact, the façade is a bizarre amalgamation of the Gothic and Renaissance styles, but its three superimposed pediments, because of their very peculiarity, succeed in creating a unified and coherent appearance. The church also contains the reliquary of the patron saint of Paris, St. Geneviève, who in 451 saved the city from the threat of the Huns.

Interior

If the façade of the church is surprising because of its composite appearance, the interior is equally so because of the architectural innovations it contains. In Gothic style with three aisles and transept, the interior has very high cylindrical piers which support the vaults and are linked together by a gallery above the arches. But the most picturesque part of the interior of the church, which makes St. Etienne unique of its kind in Paris, is the "jubé", that is, the suspended gallery which separates the nave from the choir. Possibly designed by Philibert Delorme, it is the only "jubé" known in Paris and its construction dates from between 1521 and about 1545. The splendid fretwork of Renaissance inspiration with which it is decorated continues into the spiral staircases at the sides, thus creating an uninterrupted rhythmic effect. In the ambulatory, next to the pillars of the Lady Chapel, are buried two great figures of 17th-century French literature: Pascal and Racine. The windows in the ambulatory and choir have splendid stained glass from the 16th and 17th centuries.

CHURCH OF THE SORBONNE

The church of the Sorbonne is one of the oldest parts of the university's buildings: constructed between 1635 and 1642 by Lemercier, its façade is typically Baroque, with two orders below an elegant cupola. The motif of the volutes which link the lower order to the upper is Italian in origin; a pictorial note is introduced by the passage from the columns in the lower part to the flatter pilaster strips in the upper part, which creates a gradual increase in luminosity. Inside the church, in the transept, is the white marble tomb of Cardinal Richelieu, sculpted by Girardon in 1694 to a design by Le Brun.

HÔTEL DE CLUNY

Standing next to the ruins of the Roman baths (dating from between the 2nd and the beginning of the 3rd century), this building with its green lawns and gardens is one of the finest examples of so-called International Gothic architecture in Paris. On this land, owned by the monastery of Cluny in Burgundy, the abbot Jacques d'Amboise between 1485 and 1498 had a building constructed as a resi-

dence for the Benedictine monks who came from Cluny to visit the capital. During the Revolution, the building was declared by decree to be public property and sold. In 1833 it became the residence of the collector Alexandre du Sommerand, and on his death in 1842 his home and his collections were acquired by the State. Two years later, the museum here was inaugurated, containing objects illustrating life in medieval France, ranging from costumes to goldsmiths' wares, from majolica to arms and from statues to tapestries. One enters the museum by a door which opens directly onto the courtyard. From this point, one can fully appreciate the elegance and sobriety of the building: two orders of crossed

windows and a tower with stairs adorned with the emblems of St. James. The International Gothic style is expressed here in the balustrade crowning the roof and in the dormer-windows, by now a classical motif.

The Chapel

In the twenty-four rooms of the museum are the collections which belonged to Alexandre du Sommerand and which, because of their multiplicity and wealth of material, give a complete panorama of what daily life must have been like in the Middle Ages. One of the most precious collections of the museum is that of the tapestries, woven in the Loire and in Flanders in the

15th and 16th centuries. In Room 11, also called the Rotonda, is the famous tapestry, " La Dame à la Liocorne ", from the beginning of the 16th century. On this floor of the museum, the best known and most splendid room is without doubt Room 20, that is the Chapel originally used by the abbots. In the purest of International Gothic styles, it has a single pier at the centre of the room, where the ribbing of the vault meets; along the walls are a series of corbels with niches containing the statues of the Amboise family. The finest works in the Chapel are the celebrated tapestries illustrating the Legend of St. Stephen, destined for the Cathedral of Auxerre and completed in about 1490.

ST -GERMAIN-DES-PRÉS

Here one is emerged once more in the animated life of the quarter of St. Germain, whose typical and colourful streets interweave and cross one another to form picturesque corners. Here too is the church of Sainte-Germain-des-Prés, the oldest church in Paris, built between the 11th and 12th centuries, and destroyed no less than four times in forty years by the Normans, but each time rebuilt in its severe Romanesque forms. In the façade one can see the remains of the 12th-century portal, unfortunately half-hidden by the 17th-century portico erected in 1607. The bell-tower, on the other hand, is entirely Romanesque, its corners reinforced and thickened by robust buttresses. In the 19th century, the two towers which stood at the sides of the choir were demolished, and of the choir itself there are only a few remains. The interior has three aisles and a transept, the end of which was modified in the 17th century. As a result of the restoration of the church in the 19th century, the vaults and capitals now have decorations too rich to allow the otherwise simple and severe structure of the interior fully to be appreciated. The most interesting part of the building is the choir with its ambulatory, where the original architecture of the 12th century is still in part preserved intact. In this church are the tombs of two illustrious figures: that of Cartesius, in the second chapel on the right, and that of the Polish king John Casimir, in the transept on the left.

PANTHÉON

Born as the church of Sainte Geneviève in fulfilment of a vow made by Louis XV during a serious illness in 1744, it was designed by Soufflot, begun in 1758 and completed with the contribution of Rondelet in 1789. During the Revolution it became the Temple of Glory, used for the burial of great men; under Napoleon it was reopened for worship in 1806, but only until 1885, when it returned once and for all to its status as a secular temple. Soufflot, in designing it, sought a decidedly classical style, returning to the ancient world. Its dimensions, first of all, are exceptional: 360 feet long by 272 feet high. A stairway in front of the temple leads up to a pronaos with 22 columns, which support a pediment on which in 1831 David d'Angers sculpted the allegorical work representing the Fatherland between Liberty and History. Here one can also read the famous inscription: " Aux grandes hommes, la patrie reconnaisante " (" To the great men, from their grateful fatherland "). The whole building is dominated by the great cupola, similar to Christopher Wren's dome on the church of St. Paul in London; here too, the drum is surrounded by a ring of Corinthian columns. The interior is in the form of a Greek cross, with the cupola above the crossing, supported by four piers, on one of which is the tomb of Rousseau. The walls are decorated with paintings, of which the most famous are those by Puvis de Chavannes, illustrating stories of St. Geneviève. The crypt which lies below the temple contains many tombs of illustrious men. Worth recalling are those of Victor Hugo (brought here in 1885), Emile Zola, Voltaire, the designer Soufflot himself, Carnot and Mirabeau. There are 425 steps leading up to the top of the cupola, from which there is a vast and impressive panorama.

PLACE
DES VOSGES

Looking at it from above, from one of the typical dormer-windows above the slate roofs, the square has the appearance of an enormous church cloister: perfectly square, 118 yards long on each side, it is completely closed in by thirty-six picturesque old buildings, with porticoes on the ground floor, surmounted by two orders of windows. In the square itself are green trees and flower gardens, while in the centre is a marble statue of Louis XIII on horseback, a copy of the original by P. Biard destroyed during the Revolution. The square occupies the site of the Hôtel des Tournelles, where Henry II died in a tournament in 1559. The square was designed by Henry IV in 1607 and completed in 1612. Because of its perfect form, because of the succession of porticoes which must have lent themselves to tranquil promenades and because of the gentle contrast between the green of the gardens and the severity of the surrounding buildings (buildings in which the pure white of the stone alternates with the warm red of the bricks), the square became another centre of fashionable life in the Paris which had not yet experienced the horror and violence of the Revolution. In the centre of the southern side is the Pavilion of the King, the most splendid of the buildings, reserved for Henry IV, while in front of it is the building occupied by the Queen. At number 6 is the Victor Hugo Museum, occupying the house where the great writer lived from 1832 until 1848. In it are souvenirs and objects recalling the most important moments in his life, as well as about 350 drawings which bear witness to his great and versatile genius.

MOULIN-ROUGE

Like Montparnasse, but even more so, Montmartre was and still is one of the most curious and picturesque quarters of Paris. It stands on a limestone hill 425 feet high where, according to the legend, St. Denis, the first bishop of Paris, was decapitated in 272. Some believe that the area's name derives from this fact: originally called " mons Martyrum " (Mount of the Martyrs), it later acquired its present form. Throughout the 19th century,

this was the mecca of all those artists who believed that the Bohemian life meant living freely, making one's art the main reason for living and rejecting any attempt from without to impose a way of life. Every painter, from the most famous to the most humble, has left a trace of his life and art at Montmartre. At the foot of the hill (the " butte Montmartre "), is Place Blanche, dominated by the long blades of the windmill of the Moulin Rouge (" Red Windmill "), founded in 1889, where the artists Valentin le Désossé, Jane Avril and La Goulue performed. This caba-

ret, on whose stage the " can-can " was born, is linked to the memory of the painter Toulouse-Lautrec, who passed his nights here setting down with his brush the most curious and picturesque details and the truest and most humane images of the night life of the cabarets and theatres. Here those personages who lived for art, but were excluded from the art blessed by official recognition, finally found their place. Depicted on a grand scale in the posters of Toulouse-Lautrec, they achieved a renown which they had never had on the boards of the Moulin-Rouge.

" AU LAPIN AGILE "

To understand Montmartre, to enter into the spirit of the place, one must walk along its narrow streets, see where the people live and discover for oneself its various characteristic little angles. Walking down Rue Norvins, one eventually comes to the steep and picturesque Rue Saules. In this area lived some of the most famous of the Parisian painters, among them Suzanne Vladon and Utrillo, whose paintings

recreate the " boulangeries ", the cafés, the bare trees and the deserted benches of Montmartre. On the corner of Rue Saint Vincent, half-hidden by an acacia tree, is the rustic cabaret, " Au lapin agile ", which was originally called the " Cabaret des Assassins " but which derived its present name (" At the Sign of the Agile Rabbit ") from the sign itself, painted by the artist Gill. The cabaret was immortalised by the pen and brush of writers and painters who later became famous, and literary gatherings are still held there.

SACRÉ-CŒUR

From whatever part of the city one surveys the panorama of Paris, one's eye finally comes to rest on the white domes of Sacré-Cœur. Standing majestically on the top of the hill of Montmartre, it was erected in 1876 by national subscription and consecrated in 1919. Its architects (among the most important were Abadie and Magno) designed it in a curious style which is a mixture of Romanesque and Byzantine. The four small domes and

integration of the church of Sacré-Cœur in the landscape of Paris, which is now accepted by all, may have been possible precisely because of this note of strident contrast, giving a value to the church itself and to the other monuments and throwing each one into relief within a valid historic and artistic context.

PLACE DU TERTRE

The concept of painting which was current in former times — that of the painter who lived as a painter and lived only for his painting — has changed today, but this is perhaps not true of at least one place: Place du Tertre. Not that time has stopped here: the process of change has gone on, introducing all those new personalities and new things which are an inevitable part of modern times. It would be foolish to come to Place du Tertre and the tiny streets around it looking for traces of the atmosphere of the good old days: here, as everywhere, the alterations brought by time have had their inexorable effect on man and his surroundings. But that way of painting, slow and absorbed, sitting outside on stools or small iron chairs in front of the easel — this has remained the same as it was many years ago. There are no famous monuments in this tiny, tree-lined square; one could say, instead, that the monuments are the people themselves who live and work here and who fill its narrow streets, its little old shops and smoke-filled cafés with their colourful but tranquil lives. What we see on the canvasses displayed in the square is certainly not great art, but nor is its value limited to that of the souvenir for tourist consumption. This too is a way of expressing a love for the city: to create an image on a few square inches of canvas is to immortalise the image, not only for the others but above all for oneself.

the large central dome, standing solidly on the high drum, are typically Oriental. On the back part, a square bell-tower 275 feet high contains the famous " Savoyarde ", a bell weighing no less than 19 tons and thus one of the biggest in the world. Dignified steps lead up to the façade of the church and the porch with three arches which stands in front of it; above are equestrian statues of what are perhaps the two historical figures best loved by the French, King Louis the Blessed and Joan of Arc. The interior, because of its decorations of reliefs, paintings and mosaics which in places are incredibly elaborate, can almost be said to have lost its architectural consistency. From the inside of the church, one can descend into the vast underground crypt, or else climb up to the top of the cupola, from which there is a panoramic view of the city and its surrounding areas extending for miles. In order to see the white mass of the church itself from an even better vantage point, one should descend into Place St. Pierre below, either by the convenient cable railway or down the ramps of stairs. One could perhaps object that the style of this church, its very colour and its brazenly monumental dimensions contrast too strongly with the city's other monuments and the patina of grey which they have acquired with the passing of time. But the

VERSAILLES

Versailles, which lies south-west of Paris, was a modest village until 1624, when Louis XIII had a hunting castle built there, a castle later transformed and enlarged by Louis XIV. The castle had assumed its present-day appearance by 1690, after long and complex projects carried out under the direction of Le Vau, Hardouin-Mansart and Le Nôtre, who was involved above all in the planning of the magnificent gardens. In 1682, Versailles took over the role of Paris as capital of the kingdom, Louis XIV trans-

ferring his government here as part of his plan to keep the nobles under control. From this year up until 6 October 1789, Versailles had its period of maximum splendour, basking in the pomp and ceremony of a court forgetful of the difficult conditions of the country at large, but always ready for new luxuries, endless hunting parties and magnificent banquets. On the 6th of October of that year, however, the king and his family returned to Paris in their gilded carriage, after an unprecedented demonstration in

which a procession of market women marched on Versailles. In the following period, deprived of the royal court, the castle fell into abandon; it was sacked repeatedly and many of its works of art were carried off, until in 1837 it was restored by Louis Philippe and converted into a Museum of French History. Occupied by the Germans in 1870, it was the scene of the coronation of Wilhelm of Prussia as emperor of Germany. Then in 1875 the French Republic was proclaimed here, and in 1919 it was used for the signing of the peace treaty with Germany. From the vast semi-circle of the Place d'Armes, there is a superb view of the palace, with its three successive courtyards: the first, called the Court of the Ministers, at the end of which stands the equestrian statue of Louis XIV; the second, known as the Royal Court, to which the royal carriages had access; and the third and last, called the Court of Marble, surrounded by what was the original nucleus of the castle built by Louis XIII, with red bricks alternating with white stone. From the Royal Court one can pass through an arcade to reach the western façade of the palace, the most famous and without doubt the finest of its façades. The façade extends along a front 635 yards long, opening onto a series of beautifully planned gardens. The central projecting section was designed by the architect Le Vau, while the two wings behind this, which create an effect of harmony and elegance, are the work of Hardouin-Mansart. Each section consists of two orders, the lower one of rusticated arches and the upper with piers and pilaster strips and tall windows. The two orders are surmounted by a balustraded attic storey, in which were the living quarters for the members of the enormous royal court, while the central section and the two wings were inhabited by the family of the king and the royal princes. From the Royal Court, by way of the Gabriel Wing, also called the Wing of Louis XV, one has access to the interior of the palace. This also contains the Historical Museum, in whose eleven rooms the eras of Louis XIII and Louis XIV are illustrated. From here one can go on to the Opéra, designed by Gabriel in 1770 for the marriage of Louis XVI and Marie Antoinette: oval in form, it has precious carved and gilded woodwork on a blue

background. On the second floor, the Chapel, designed by Hardouin-Mansart and built between 1698 and 1710, merits special attention. It has three aisles and square piers which support the arches, surmounted by a gallery with fluted columns. While still on this floor, one can admire the six large rooms of the " Grand Appartement ", or Suite of the King, where the sovereign received his court three times a week, from six till ten o'clock in the evening; the Apartment of the King, with the room where Louis XIV died in 1715; and the " Grand

Appartement " of the Queen, the scene of a bloody encounter between the guards of Marie Antoinette and a group of insurgents on the morning of 6 October 1798. But the most luxurious wing of the palace is the *Gallery of Mirrors,* access to which is through the Hall of War. The masterpiece of Hardouin-Mansart, who supervised its construction in 1678, it is 246 feet long and 33 feet wide and its vault is decorated with paintings by Le Brun celebrating French victories. Its fame and beauty derive from the seventeen large windows which look out onto

the park, corresponding to a similar number of mirrors on the opposite wall, so that the whole gallery is flooded with light and the peaceful green of the gardens seems actually to penetrate silently into the interior of the palace itself.

The gardens of Versailles, which deserve to be treated separately, are rightly considered the prototype of the French-style garden, due to their elegant design which is never excessive and yet contains a wealth of artistic devices and scenic inventions. Designed by Le Nôtre between 1661 and 1668, the gardens occupy an area of some 250 acres and constitute an integral part of and logical complement to the palace. Their design is subject to strict geometric principles, but despite this there is no danger of monotony in the continually varied perspective created by flower-beds, wooded areas, statues and fountains with their jets of water in every part of the vast park. Descending the central terrace, one encounters the masterpiece of Marsy in the Fountain of Latona, in which the goddess in depicted with her son and daughter, Apollo and Diana, dominating the concentric basins with their pyramidal form. This fountain stands at the beginning of the long Avenue of Tapis-Vert which leads to the large *Fountain of Apollo*. In this work, Tuby imagined the chariot of the god as being pulled by four horses, emerging in imperious style from the water, while tritons blow on their shells to announce the god's arrival. Behind this sculptural group — which, with its impetuous and yet majestic effect, stands almost as a symbol of the whole era of Versailles' maximum splendour — is a vast green area, through which runs the Grand Canal, more than a mile long, met halfway along its course by the Small Canal. Frequently imitated during the following centuries by the courts of other countries, Versailles remains the most limpid evidence of the high degree of artistic maturity attained in this epoch.

INDEX